Albert Schmitz
Edith Schmitz

TOOLBOX

ENGLISH

for

Technical Purposes

1
Coursebook

D1727452

Max Hueber Verlag

Folgende Symbole werden verwendet:

 für Texte auf der Cassette

 für Texte auf der CD (hier CD 1, Text 2)

3. 2. 1. | Die letzten Ziffern
1999 98 97 96 95 | bezeichnen Zahl und Jahr des Druckes.
Alle Drucke dieser Auflage können, da unverändert, nebeneinander
benutzt werden.
1. Auflage
© 1995 Max Hueber Verlag, D-85737 Ismaning
Sprachliche Durchsicht und Beratung: Eileen Anne Plümer
Verlagsredaktion: Cornelia Dietz, München
Zeichnungen: Paul Netzer, Berlin
Herstellung/Layout/Umschlag: Alois Sigl, München
Druck und Bindung: Ludwig Auer GmbH, Donauwörth
Printed in Germany
ISBN 3-19-002416-2

Vorwort

Toolbox ist ein neues Lehrwerk für technisches Englisch, das sich an Lernende aus den verschiedensten technischen Berufen richtet, aber auch für diejenigen geeignet ist, die sich noch in einer technischen Ausbildung befinden. Die Arbeit mit **Toolbox 1** setzt Grundkenntnisse voraus, die etwa 1–2 Jahren Englischunterricht entsprechen („falsche Anfänger"). Um Teilnehmern und Teilnehmerinnen mit sehr geringen Vorkenntnissen den Einstieg zu erleichtern, ist dem *Workbook* zu **Toolbox 1** eine Grundgrammatik vorgeschaltet, mit deren Hilfe die elementaren Strukturen wiederholt und geübt werden können. Die Units des Lehrwerks führen in technische Zusammenhänge ein und bieten einen leichten, abgestuften Einstieg in die Sprache des technischen Englisch. **Toolbox 1** und **Toolbox 2** eignen sich zur Vorbereitung auf das ICC Certificate „English for Technical Purposes".

Die technisch orientierten Texte, Dialoge und Übungen stammen aus unterschiedlichen Fachgebieten, z. B. aus den Bereichen Computer, Elektronik, Maschinenbau, Werkstoffe, Verfahrenstechnik, Bauwesen, Papierherstellung, Forschung und Wissenschaft, Meß- und Regeltechnik, Ökologie und Umweltschutz, Automobilbau oder Energie. Die Textsorten umfassen hauptsächlich Sachtexte, wie etwa Beschreibungen von Maschinen oder technischen Abläufen.

Toolbox legt besonderen Wert auf den Umgang mit der modernen technischen Sprache, sowohl im mündlichen als auch im schriftlichen Bereich. Alle vier Fertigkeiten (Hören, Lesen, Sprechen, Schreiben) werden gleichermaßen geübt.

- Die Cassetten/CDs zum *Coursebook* enthalten Hörverständnisübungen zu jeder Unit; zur Kontrolle befinden sich die entsprechenden Tapescripts im Anhang des *Teacher's Book*. Auf den Cassetten/CDs sind auch die Lektionslesetexte und die „Language Functions" verfügbar. Zum *Workbook* wird eine gesonderte Cassette mit weiteren Hörverständnisübungen angeboten (Tapescripts im Anhang).

- Die Lektionslesetexte sorgen dafür, daß die Kursteilnehmer und -teilnehmerinnen genügend Gelegenheit bekommen, die für technische Berufe überaus wichtige Fertigkeit „Lesen" einzuüben.

- Zum Trainieren der Sprechfertigkeit gibt es Telefongespräche, Reklamationen und Bestellungen, Fachgespräche, aber auch Dialoge aus dem Alltag. Hierfür werden nützliche Redemittel angeboten.

- Im schriftlichen Bereich werden z. B. das Schreiben von Briefen, das Erstellen von Protokollen sowie das „note-taking" geübt.

Verfasser und Verlag

Contents

Testing Your Language – Part Two

Appendix

Jobs and tools – an introduction

1

Have a look at the jobs shown on the computer screen. Is your job shown there, too? Or are you an apprentice? Or a trainee? Why do you want to learn technical English? (Read letters? Speak with other people? Make telephone calls? Read instructions and specifications? Read technical journals? Discuss technical problems with other technicians and engineers? Write reports and letters to English or American companies? Read owner's manuals? Talk to English or American customers?)

- Automotive Engineer
- Chemical Engineer
- Civil Engineer
- Electrical Engineer
- Electrician
- Locksmith
- Mechanic
- Mechanical Engineer
- Papermaker
- Process Engineer
- Programmer
- Sales Engineer
- Systems Analyst
- Technician
- Technical Draughtsman
- Toolmaker

Modern production with CIM ...

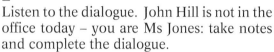

CIM MODEL

DESIGN ENGINEERING

SALES - ORDERS

PRODUCTION ENGINEERING AND QA

PRODUCTION PLANNING AND CONTROL

PRODUCT CENTRES

MANUFACTURING/ PRODUCT SUPPORT

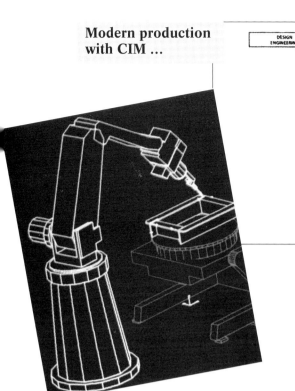

... industrial robots ...

... and CAD.

2

Listen to the dialogue. John Hill is not in the office today – you are Ms Jones: take notes and complete the dialogue.

Complaining about the hardware

Ms Jones: ...

Mr Keats: Hello. May I speak to John Hill, please?

Ms Jones: ...

Mr Keats: Well ... I'm Tom Keats of the Chesterfield Motor Corporation.

Ms Jones: ...

Mr Keats: You see, John Hill helped us install your new LAN network, and now we're having a bit of trouble.

Ms Jones: ...

Mr Keats: Well, I don't know exactly, but there seems to be something wrong with the hardware.

Ms Jones: ...

Mr Keats: All right – but tell him it's urgent. Good-bye.

Ms Jones: ...

3

Which explanation belongs to which drawing (1 to 12)?

a. Pliers are used for holding, bending, or cutting things.

b. The vice shown in the picture is made of cast-iron.

c. The screwdriver bits fit in every power drill.

d. Hole saws are used for making large holes in wood or plastic.

e. This is a bench grinder – useful for sharpening and polishing.

f. This table saw gives you a work area of 44" x 27".

g. A drill press with 12 speeds – every workshop must have one.

h. Spanners (US: wrenches) are used for turning nuts and bolts.

i. Before you drill a hole, you must use a centre punch.

j. A file is a tool with a rough surface.

k. This high-speed steel bit is ideal for steel and cast-iron.

l. Metal shears are used for cutting sheet metal.

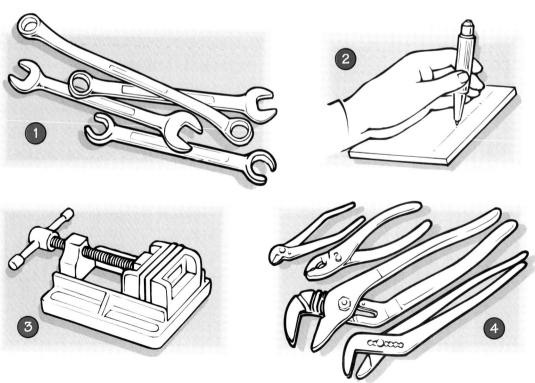

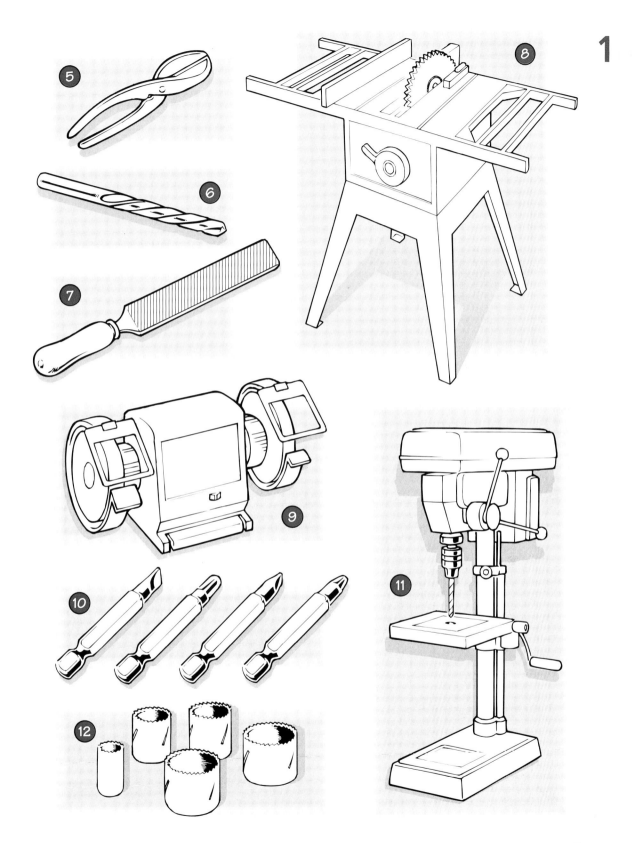

A LOOK AT GRAMMAR:
Passive (1)

Active	Passive
I'm sure we can repair the bench saw.	I'm sure the bench saw can be repaired.
We can discuss the problem now.	The problem can be discussed now.
We can install the new computer system.	The new computer system can be installed.
They can check the bench grinder.	The bench grinder can be checked.

Turn the small gear wheel anti-clockwise.

Which way will the big wheel on the left turn?

4

Complete the sentences below by putting in *don't* or *can't*:

LANGUAGE FUNCTIONS:

Things not to do
Negative statements

a. ... write the report in German!

b. These pliers ... be used for metal parts.

c. The computer ... be installed today.

d. If you find the technical journals, ... throw them away.

e. Why ... you want to read the owner's manual in English?

f. I ... know if this vice is made of cast-iron or steel.

5
Listening and note-taking.

Situation:
Ms Jenkins is phoning "World of Tools". She wants to order some goods for her company. Listen carefully and take notes.

```
WORLD OF TOOLS
29 Two Springs Road
Chesterfield, Derbyshire S40 3RR
Tel: 0246 82934
Fax: 0246 82417          ORDER FORM
```

Name: _____

Address: _____

Tel: _____

Fax: _____

How Many	Catalogue No.	Size	Colour	Page	Description	Price

Method of Payment:
- ☐ Cheque
- ☐ Credit Card

Total ▢

Finding the right tool …

Dear John,

I'm really looking forward to seeing you next summer. You know this will be my first RV holiday (or "vacation", as you say in the States), so I'm a little worried about some technical details, such as the LPgas system. Could you try to get an RV manual for me? I would appreciate this very much.

Best wishes,

Michael

1

Discussion.
Have a look at Michael's postcard on the left and the explanations from the
RV manual below.
What is your opinion about an RV holiday?
What do you think are the advantages / disadvantages?
Which countries would you like to see in an RV? (Give reasons.)
Do you think an RV holiday is cheaper than a "normal" holiday? (Explain.)
Can you think of some technical problems people might have (electrical system /
gas / driving / traffic / maintenance)?

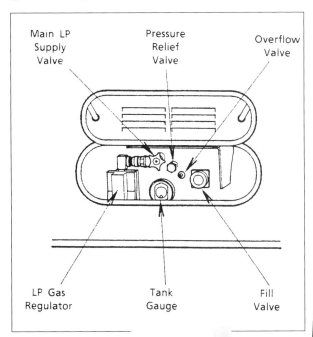

Main LP Supply Valve · Pressure Relief Valve · Overflow Valve · LP Gas Regulator · Tank Gauge · Fill Valve

WARNING

DO NOT FILL CONTAINER TO MORE THAN 80 PERCENT OF CAPACITY. Make sure the motor home is level when filling. It is possible to accidentally overfill the tank if the vehicle is unlevel, with the fill valve on the uphill side. Overfilling the LP gas tank can result in uncontrolled gas flow, which can cause fire or explosion. A properly filled container will contain approximately 80 percent of its volume as liquid LP gas.

All pilot lights must be extinguished and supply valve closed before refilling LP gas tanks or vehicle fuel tanks.

Do not smoke or expose an open flame while near an LP refueling area. LP gas is heavier-than-air and extremely flammable.

Never use an open flame to test for LP gas leaks.

Replace all protective covers and caps on LP system after filling.

Never fill the LP tank with engine or generator running.

Dimensions and Capacities

Overall Length	20'2"
Overall Height	9'5"
Overall Width	96"
Interior Height	81"
Interior Width	91-1/4"
Fresh Water – Gallons	28
Waste Water – Gallons	35
LP Tanks – Lbs	60
Fuel Tank – Gallons	33

Passive (2)

Active	**Passive**
They build the engines in Coventry.	The engines are built in Coventry.
They speak English here.	English is spoken here.
They make these holes with a drilling machine.	These holes are made with a drilling machine.
They publish the books in German and English.	The books are published in German and English.

NOTE: If something is going on at the moment, the -ing form is usually used:
The car is being repaired. = They are repairing the car at the moment.

2
Make sentences:

publish / manual / English and French
→ The manual is published in English and French.

a. make / machine parts / London

b. print / book / England

c. build / machines / robots

d. read / technical journals / engineers

e. move / work table / up and down

3
Try to finish the following sentences:

a. A fire can be caused by …

b. When the LP gas tank is overfilled …

c. Before refilling LP gas tanks …

d. An open flame should never be used …

 ### 4
Listen to the dialogue and try to find the missing information:

Making an appointment

a. The extension is …

b. John Hill is having some trouble with …

c. …would be fine.

d. John will be there in the … at about …

Group work. Write down a similar dialogue and practise it in the group.

Writing a message. You are Tom Keats. You will not be in the office next Monday morning. Write down a short message for Helen White, a colleague of yours. Tell her why you will not be in the office, who will come, and what you would like her to do.

5

Have another look at the grammar explanations of Unit 1 (p. 10) and Unit 2 (p. 14). Complete the sentences below by putting in *are, be* or *can be*:

a. I'm sure the bench drill … repaired.

b. Our manuals … always printed in English.

c. This computer cannot … used for CAD.

d. This book … translated by an engineer.

e. That's a very old machine. Do you really think it … repaired?

f. Metal shears … never used for cutting paper.

6

Put in *in, for,* or *to*:

a. Are you interested … computers?

b. Do you often write letters … your friends?

c. Who is this journal … ?

d. Is it possible … overfill the tank?

e. They use "gallons" … the USA, not "litres".

7

Have another look at the texts of this unit (including "Language Functions" on the right) and complete the sentences below by putting in the correct preposition:

a. She was a little worried … the LP gas system.

b. I'm really looking forward … that party on Saturday.

c. You must not fill the container … more than 80 percent of capacity.

d. He will try … get an RV manual for me.

e. Do you like travelling … a motorhome or a van conversion?

f. She introduced me … the marketing director last week.

g. Perhaps I should start … introducing my colleagues.

h. What do you think are the advantages … an RV holiday?

LANGUAGE FUNCTIONS: 🔊 ①⑥

Introductions and greetings
Addressing someone

Excuse me, is this seat taken? – No, it isn't.

Mr Smith! – Yes, can I help you?

You're new to the company, aren't you?

May I introduce our Sales Engineer?

Mr Miller, may I introduce you to Ms Jones? – How d'you do, Ms Jones. – How d'you do. (Pleased to meet you.)

Allow me to introduce our Marketing Director.

May I introduce myself?

Perhaps I should start by introducing myself.

8

Recently, Deirdre Buchanon bought a van conversion. Listen to her conversation with a neighbour, Mr Greenfield, and try to find the missing words below:

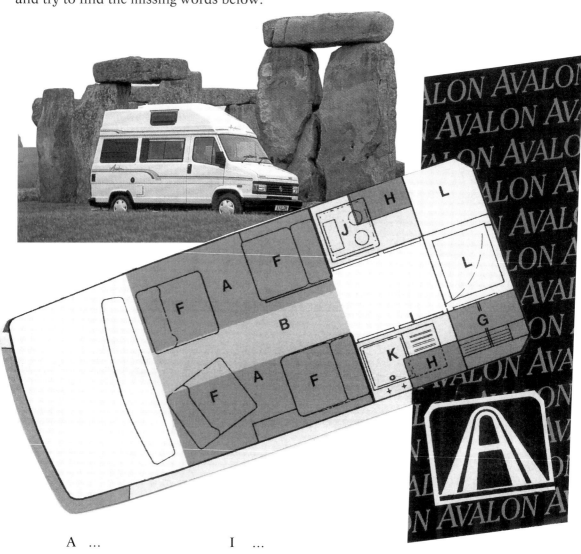

A ...	I ...
B ...	J Cooker grill oven
F Dinette seat	K Sink drainer
G Wardrobe	L ...
H ...	

Designing and drawing

1

Discussion: Do you think a good design is really so important? (Why? / Why not?) Can you think of some modern products with a very good design? (Cars? Airplanes? Electric shavers? Hi-fi equipment? Computers? Typewriters?) If yes, what do you like about the design? Do you think it is easier to sell products with a good design?

3

2

Listen to the dialogue and try to find the missing information:

Booking a flight

a. Passenger's name: ... / Passenger's phone number: ...

b. Airline: ... / Flight from ... to ...

c. Time of departure: ...

A LOOK AT GRAMMAR:

Passive (3)

Active	**Passive**
They must change the gear wheel.	The gear wheel must be changed.
They must clean all the tools.	All the tools must be cleaned.
We must write reports and letters.	Reports and letters must be written.
You must never use open flames.	Open flames must never be used.

Active	**Passive**
We will discuss the problem next week.	The problem will be discussed next week.
They will use a LAN network.	A LAN network will be used.
We will put the table near the window.	The table will be put near the window.

3

Engineering drawing standards

In our modern technological society, common drawing standards are necessary to avoid confusion in industry and commerce. Booklets are published explaining the standards that have been agreed on in this country by the British Standards Institute. The following pages illustrate some of the engineering drawing standards which are useful when making a working drawing:

TYPES OF LINE USED

Outlines

For dimensions, projection and hatching lines

For hidden details

For centre lines

Section lines

To represent a break

PRINTING

When printing letters and numbers it is important that they can be clearly seen; printing is therefore recommended.

ABCDEFGHIJKLM
NOPQRSTUVWXYZ
123456789

Examples of good and bad printing

20 mm   20 mm
SECTION   secTioN

DIMENSIONING

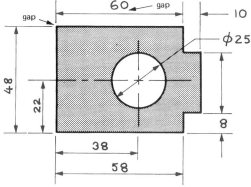

Dimensioned according to British Standards

Dimensioning radii, circles and holes

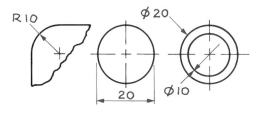

Dimensioning pictorial views

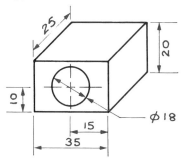

Thread conventions

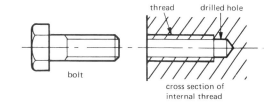

bolt

thread   drilled hole

cross section of internal thread

Cross section of a wheel and washer

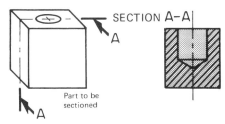

grub screw

shaft

Section X–X

Notes about cross-sectioning

• Shafts and bolts are not sectioned.
• Adjoining parts (the washer and wheel) are cross-sectioned in opposite directions as shown above.

Sectioning

Sectioning allows us to show what an object would look like inside if cut. Below are examples: solid parts are cross-hatched at 45 degrees. Lines A–A and B–B indicate where the object is sectioned. A few things such as holes, nuts and bolts are not sectioned.

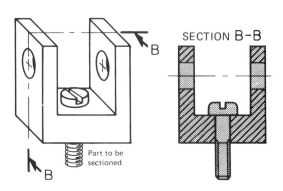

SECTION A–A

A

Part to be sectioned

A

Section shows depth of drilled hole.

SECTION B–B

B

Part to be sectioned

B

3

Questions
about the 'door bolt' drawing below

a. Identify the 'front view' (which is cross-sectioned), the 'end view' and the 'plan'.
b. What scale is used for this drawing?
c. What extra information could be added to this drawing?

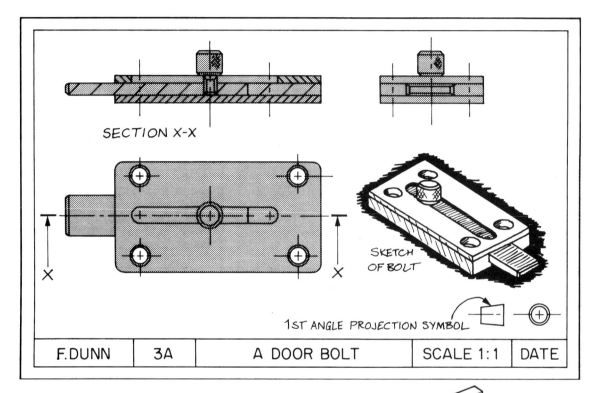

SECTION X-X

SKETCH OF BOLT

1ST ANGLE PROJECTION SYMBOL

| F.DUNN | 3A | A DOOR BOLT | SCALE 1:1 | DATE |

4

Group work. In groups of three or four, make a list of some simple objects you could design.
After some minutes, each group chooses one object and makes a design.
Compare the results and discuss the different designs.

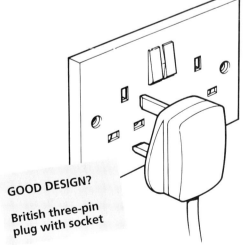

GOOD DESIGN?

British three-pin plug with socket

5

Have another look at the grammar explanations of Unit 1 (p. 10) and Unit 2 (p. 14) and the "Language Functions" on the right. Change the sentences below into the passive:

a. We must test the material.

b. How can we test the plugs?

c. They design the plugs in Great Britain.

d. We have just signed a new contract.

e. She cuts the paper into little pieces.

f. They must deliver the goods now.

g. We can improve the drawings.

h. You must make a ring.

i. We do not section bolts.

j. We must clean the engine.

k. He can make the drawings on a computer.

l. You must report the accident.

LANGUAGE FUNCTIONS:

How to express your feelings

We've just signed a new million-dollar contract with the Indonesian steel company. – That *is* good news!

It would have been nice to meet him before he leaves.

He's just lost his job. – How terrible for him!

I must say I had hoped for an earlier delivery.

When I came to this company ten years ago, I didn't know a word of English. – It must have been very difficult for you.

She had an accident last week – broke her arm, I think. – I'm extremely sorry to hear that.

MÖBIUS, August Ferdinand (1790-1868)

German mathematician and astronomer; inventor of the Möbius strip

6

Listen and take notes. The four short texts you will hear are in the correct order (a to d), but not the drawings (1 to 4). Decide which drawing belongs to which text. Make some Möbius strips and see what happens.

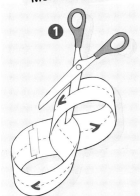

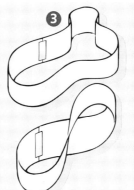

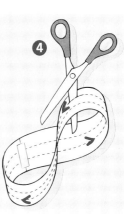

1

Situation:
Two people ("A" and "B" on the recording) are talking about space travel – for and against.
Listen carefully to the texts and take notes (as shown below).

Group work. Make a list of some of the things you think have been developed thanks to space research and space travel. Compare the list with the lists made by the other groups and discuss the result.

International Telecommunications

If you telephone someone in the USA from Britain, the message is often transmitted as radio waves instead of travelling along a wire. It cannot be beamed straight between two countries because the earth is round. So it is beamed up to a communications satellite, using a dish, and then beamed back down to earth. The message travels about 72,000 km and takes about a quarter of a second.

There are many different communications satellites, each stationed above a different part of the world. Small parabolic dishes are now available which can be installed outside individual houses to receive the broadcast directly from the satellite.

2

Look at the text above and the "Language Functions" on the right and decide which word must be used to fill the gap:

a. The broadcast was … at 10.00 p.m.

b. They have a little workshop where they repair … appliances such as radios, TV sets and cassette recorders.

c. Glass is a very … material.

d. A … is a rounded glass lamp that fits into an electrical socket.

e. The radio … was beamed to Europe from Denver in the United States.

f. Hubble's two solar panels operate on just 110–150 watts, the power of a common household light … .

g. The volume of universe that can be observed with the Hubble … is 350 times greater than that of Earth-based telescopes.

LANGUAGE FUNCTIONS:

1
13

Forbidding something

I'm sorry but we can't allow unaccompanied visitors in the plant.

You're not allowed to smoke in here.

He wanted to take over the other company but the Board of Directors wouldn't allow it.

This material mustn't be used for electrical installations.

I wonder if you'd mind not touching that light bulb – it's quite fragile.

Stop making such a noise – we're trying to concentrate.

Do not park here.

Telescope will seek planets of other suns

NASA scientists checked again and again – and finally it was ready for the launch into space: the $1.5 billion Hubble space telescope. Hubble will relay pictures to NASA stations, and every astronomer can use the information. Will Hubble bring us closer to answering the question: Are there planets beyond our solar system?

"We want Hubble to look into regions of total darkness, to look where nobody has ever looked," said a scientist. Whether life could exist there would be another matter. Hubble would not be able to get close enough to tell. "If you ask two scientists, 'How many planets are there in the galaxy with life on them?' you may get answers ranging from none to lots," explained a Texas astronomer from San Antonio.

3
Questions on the text.

Who developed "Hubble"?

What do they want to get from the space telescope?

Who can use the information?

What does the text say about life on other planets?

Will "Hubble" give us all the answers?

What do astronomers say about life on other planets?

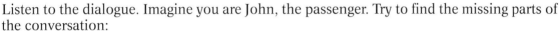

"would"

He didn't ask me. – No, but I thought he would. (= *he would do it*)

Would you hand me the wrench, please?

I'd like to make a couple of phone calls before I go to Stratford-upon-Avon. (= *I would like …*)

She would do it if she could.

4

Listen to the dialogue. Imagine you are John, the passenger. Try to find the missing parts of the conversation:

Dialogue in a taxi

John: …

Taxi Driver: Morning.

John: …

Taxi Driver: Dagenham? Ford Motor Company?

John: …

Taxi Driver: All right, but it's going to take a while – lot's of traffic this time of the day.

John: …

Taxi Driver: I think so.

John: …

Taxi Driver: First time in London?

John: …

Taxi Driver: Manchester? Sister of mine
                    lives there. Ashton-under-Lyne,
                    as a matter of fact.

John: …

Taxi Driver: About six miles or so, I
                    remember – I was there last year …

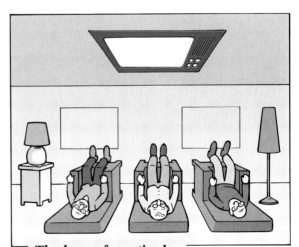

The home for retired astronauts

1

Discussion. The Eurotunnel consists of two rail tunnels and, running between and linked to them, a service tunnel for ventilation and maintenance. Each of the tunnels is about 50 kilometres long. The "mole" shown above was one of the machines used for tunnelling work. When the tunnel project was discussed, three alternative proposals were made:

- Artificial islands about five miles from the coasts; bridges between the islands and the coasts, and a tunnel between the islands.

- A bridge from coast to coast.

- A road tunnel.

What do you think of these ideas? What are the advantages / disadvantages?

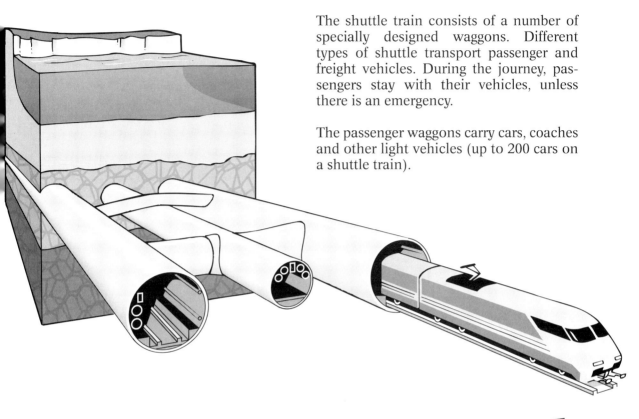

The shuttle train consists of a number of specially designed waggons. Different types of shuttle transport passenger and freight vehicles. During the journey, passengers stay with their vehicles, unless there is an emergency.

The passenger waggons carry cars, coaches and other light vehicles (up to 200 cars on a shuttle train).

2
Pair work.

On your firm's construction site you see a worker who is not wearing a helmet. Show him the sign and talk to him – tell him about the dangers involved and the regulations. Think of other safety precautions on building sites.

THIS IS A HARD HAT AREA
HELMETS MUST BE WORN AT ALL TIMES

5

Meet the man in the mole

There are many people helping to dig a tunnel, and we are going to meet one of the drivers of the tunnel boring machines. His name is Graham Milton, and he has a very important and difficult job …

Graham Milton has driven moles in different parts of the world for the past twenty years. His last job was in Egypt. The Euro-tunnel mole is the most complicated one that Graham has ever driven, and it is also the longest – two hundred and forty metres long! The moles are steered using lasers connected by satellites in space. It is clear that such moles cost a great deal of money.

Graham's day starts at seven a.m. when he is taken by bus to the entry-point. There he takes a ride on one of the service trains down to the mole. He climbs into the mole's control room and takes over from the other driver who has been working through the night. The control room is usually at the front of a mole just behind the cutting head. It is very hot and humid in a tunnel – a bit like being in a greenhouse on a sunny day!

Graham Milton works for eight hours non stop, his tea and sandwiches being sent to him on a service train.

A computer controls all the steering, and Graham checks all the workings of the boring machine. He makes sure that all of the rock is being carried away on the conveyor belt. If there is a flood in the tunnel as it is being dug, special safety precautions go into operation.

There was a total of eleven moles working on the tunnels, six working towards each other under the sea, and five more digging the links to the terminals. The target speed for digging the service tunnel was 90 metres per week on both sides (total 180 metres). The tunnel was designed so that the shuttles and British and French trains can all pass through safely, picking up their electric power from above. And some day there may even be a road tunnel – and more work for Graham Milton.

3

Read the article above and answer
the following questions by marking a, b, c, or d:

1. The mole Graham Milton drove

    a. came from Egypt.
    b. was constructed with the help of a laser.
    c. was rather complicated.
    d. was used in Egypt.

2. When Graham Milton arrived at the tunnel
site, he first

    a. took a bus to the service train.
    b. took a service train to the mole.
    c. went to the control room.
    d. went to the front of the mole.

3. The conveyor belt was used to

    a. bring equipment into the tunnel.
    b. bring the sandwiches to Graham Milton.
    c. carry the rocks out of the tunnel.
    d. move the mole into the tunnel.

4. Special safety precautions went into
operation if

    a. Graham Milton used the laser.
    b. rock was falling down.
    c. the conveyor was running.
    d. water came into the tunnel.

5. The service tunnel

    a. is used for the shuttles and the trains.
    b. was dug by eleven moles.
    c. was not dug by Graham Milton.
    d. was the first to be finished.

4
Discussion.
What do you think about Graham Milton's work? (Difficult? Dangerous?)
Have you ever done any dangerous work? (Where?)
What do you think about shift work?
Have you ever worked in shifts? (When? Where? What did you do?)
Is the night shift the worst?

5

Talking about the computer

Listen to the dialogue. Take notes of what the people are saying. Write a similar dialogue
(with another student) and introduce it to the class.

Discussion. Do you sometimes have problems with computers?

"The channel tunnel
should ease the housing
problem."

5

LANGUAGE FUNCTIONS:

Complaining
Making complaints (1)

The trouble with this job is that there is too much overtime.

The trouble is this computer works with a different operating system.

What's the trouble? – The plug doesn't fit.

There seems to be some trouble with the CPU. – Well, in that case we'll have to call in a service technician.

The engine? No, it isn't the engine, it's the starter that doesn't work.

The probability of failure will be very high if you use this sort of switch.

6

Look at the "Language Functions" on the left and complete the following sentences by putting in *complaint, failure* or *trouble*:

a. My … to arrive on time caused a lot of problems.
b. The ship was in … and signalled for help.
c. I'm having … with my computer. Can you help me?
d. The police received several …s about the pollution coming from our factory.
e. The … with your plan is that it is far too expensive.
f. The recent power … in our town was caused by a heavy storm.
g. No, they were not happy with our machines – in fact, they sent us a letter of … .

A LOOK AT GRAMMAR:

"Have got"

Instead of *have*, the expression *have got* is usually used to talk about possessions, people and things, or to describe a temporary situation:

I've got a flat in Manchester.
She's got a large house in London.
New York has got a lot of skyscrapers.
My brother's got a workshop in Hull.
Have you got a new car?

My sister's got black hair.
My dog's got very long ears.
I've got a headache.
Have you got a screwdriver for me?
She's got a book in her hand.

7

Situation: Mary and John are being interviewed about the Channel Tunnel. Listen to the interview and try to find the missing information:

a. The tunnel is important for … .
b. When the weather is bad, … are interrupted.
c. It is less expensive to … .
d. The longest tunnel in the world is in … . It is … kilometres long.
e. The Channel Tunnel is … kilometres long.

When you have done this, listen again to the interview. Take notes and write a short report on what the people are saying.

All trains will be monitored by modern control equipment. At peak times, passenger shuttle trains will depart about every 12 minutes.

Pumping oil out of the ground

1

Situation:
Michael is visiting his friend Michelle, an engineering student from Montreal. At the moment they are travelling through Alberta, one of the Canadian prairie provinces. Most of this land is covered with fields of grain. Listen to their conversation and answer the following questions:

a. How are they travelling?

b. What was it that Michael saw moving up and down?

   What do these machines do?

c. What is crude oil? (It is also called "petroleum".)

d. What will the oil companies do if an oil field is far from any town?

e. What does Michelle say about the town called Fort McMurray?

Horsehead pumps are common in Canada. The "horsehead" is the curved part at the end of the arm of an oil well pump – it keeps the cable attached between the arm and the pump rods.

Modal auxiliaries

I used to work a lot of overtime, but now I try to get home a bit earlier.
I didn't use to like using a computer, but now I enjoy it very much.
Didn't you use to write your own programs for word processing and CAD?

Every evening at half past five he will say "let's call it a day" and go home.

She must be the new sales engineer.
She looks tired – she must have been working really hard for the last few weeks.
"Have you finished that report yet?" – "You must be joking! I've hardly even started it."
Let's have a look – I think they will have finished by now.
There has to be some reason for this failure – we must find it!

LANGUAGE FUNCTIONS:

Complaining
Making complaints (2)

If you'd checked the new transmission thoroughly, we wouldn't have so much trouble now.
If you'd done it better, you wouldn't have any complaints.
You shouldn't have done it that way.
Well, they could have helped me instead of just sitting there and complaining.
It's rather noisy in here, I must say – it used to be quieter.
There's something wrong with the CAD program, I'm afraid.
That's not what we ordered.
Two of the six drill bits you sent us are defective.

2
Questions.
Where can you find a sign like the one shown below?
What does it mean?
Where else would you expect to find magnetic stripes?
What can they be used for?
Will there be more in the future? (Where?)

If your ticket has a magnetic stripe, please use the gates

3
Look again at the "Language Functions" of Unit 5 (p. 30) and Unit 6 (p. 32).
Can you write a short letter of complaint to a company?
Tell them what went wrong and what you want them to do.
Tell them it is urgent.

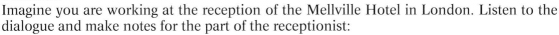

4

Situation:

Imagine you are working at the reception of the Mellville Hotel in London. Listen to the dialogue and make notes for the part of the receptionist:

Phoning a friend

Reception:	…
John:	Good morning. May I speak to Mr Svensson, please?
Reception:	…
John:	Svensson, Mats Svensson.
Reception:	…
John:	S-V-E-N-S-S-O-N.
Reception:	…

5

Have another look at the grammar explanations of this unit, particularly the structure *used to* (= we did this in the past but we don't do it now). Make sentences according to this example:

I start work at 8.30. (9 / work in Birmingham) ➔ I used to start work at 9 when I worked in Birmingham.

a. We have a lunch break at 12. (12.30 / work in the old workshop)
b. They have no complaints this year. (a lot of complaints / last year)
c. She buys the tickets at the end of the month. (at the beginning of the month / live in England)
d. I go home at 4.30. (6 / work for the Channel Tunnel project)
e. They take their holiday in June. (January / live in New Zealand)

OFFICE TIMETABLE

9.00	STARTING TIME
9.30	ARRIVE
9.45	COFFEE BREAK
11.00	WORK BREAK
11.15	PREPARE FOR LUNCH
12.00	LUNCH
2.45	AFTERNOON WORK BREAK
3.00	TEA BREAK
4.00	PREPARE TO GO HOME
4.30	GO HOME
5.00	LEAVING TIME

1

Group work. Read the text below and on the opposite page carefully and answer the following questions:

- What does the text say about the greenhouse effect?
- Are Canadians interested in environmental problems? (In what way?)
- How do consumers react?
- What does the text say about the garbage problem in Canada?
- What information do you get about the Great Lakes area?
- Where does a lot of the emissions in the Great Lakes area come from?

Canadians and Their Environment

No doubt, the planet's environment is in trouble. Possibly the most serious threat comes from the destruction of the ozone layer, that thin, invisible screen of gases high above. That natural shield is under constant attack by chemicals that are used every day in refrigeration, air conditioning and some aerosol cans and foam plastics. Another big environmental threat is that of climate warming caused by the greenhouse effect. Canada held one of the major meetings on this problem a few years ago, a conference called "The Changing Atmosphere". The experts said that carbon dioxide emissions should be cut in half in order to stop climate change.

Making the environment healthier

Canadians are also taking personal responsibility for cleaning up the environment. In many parts of the country people are now separating the garbage so that valuable wastes can be recycled. Surveys have shown that Canadians want to be able to buy products that do not harm the environment. Four out of five people would even pay as much as ten percent more for such goods. Some time ago, a special programme was launched to help consumers find products that are free of dangerous chemicals. The first three products in this group are motor oil, insulation made from recycled paper, and some products made from recycled plastic.

Cleaning Canada's lakes

Some years ago, Lake Erie, one of the Great Lakes, was so polluted with sewage and fertilizers that it was dying. Since then, Canada has spent billions of dollars on sewage treatment to reduce pollution to the Great Lakes, and the United States has spent even more.

Canada is now in the middle of an acid-rain reduction programme in the eastern half of the country, where the problem is particularly bad.

Emissions from copper and nickel plants, coal-burning power stations and cars are all being cleaned up.

A LOOK AT GRAMMAR:

Modal auxiliaries

I'm not happy with our new supplier – last month they were not able to deliver on time.
Only digital technology could have produced such a sophisticated machine.

We ought to have tested the new equipment first.
She oughtn't to complain so much.

You had better go to work now. (= *it would be better if ...*)
I'd better not switch the machine on before I've read the operating manual.
Hadn't you better use aluminium for this part? (= *wouldn't it be better if ...*)
We'd better ask the chief engineer first, hadn't we?
You'd better be careful – there's some pretty high voltage in those wires.

2
Put in *better* or *more*:

a. ... of them were coming than we expected.

b. This is a lot ... difficult than I thought.

c. Hadn't we ... check the air conditioning?

d. That new printer is much ... expensive than the old one.

e. We'd ... be careful – that's a dangerous chemical.

3
Make sentences according to the example:
go / work ➔ You'd better go to work now.

a. clean / printer
b. ask / chief engineer
c. switch off / machine
d. check / thermometer
e. have a look / manual
f. write / that report
g. call / Martin
h. finish / drawing
i. fill / tank
j. go / ticket office

4

Listen to the dialogue and answer the following questions:

Breakfast at Munchies

a. Where are John and Mats?

b. Does Mats like the hotel he's staying at?

c. What is the weather like?

d. What are they planning to do?

e. Will they go by train or by car?

Pair work. Write down a short note for a colleague. Tell him / her where you are and when you will be back at the hotel.

LANGUAGE FUNCTIONS:

Meeting other people

Would you mind coming this way?

Come this way, will you?

I wonder if I might ask you to have another look at the hardware.

What's your opinion on this?

Let's have a look at the drawing, shall we?

Would eight o'clock be convenient?

May I recommend "Munchies"?

We'd better have breakfast here in London.

You could try the orange juice – it's excellent.

5

Have another look at the grammar ("Modal auxiliaries", p. 35) and the "Language Functions" on the left and complete the sentences below by putting in *able, could* or *ought*:

a. We … to have discussed the problem at the meeting last week.

b. Do you think we will be … to get a good price for that machine?

c. I … not do it without his help.

d. I think we … to get a new drilling machine – this one's much too old.

e. Canadians want to be … to buy products that do not harm the environment.

f. The acid-rain reduction program … be very successful.

g. They … to have cleaned up the lakes years ago.

h. We … go by train – it's better for the environment.

6

Discussion.
Have a look at the photos on this page.
What do they show?

Is our environment really in such a bad
shape?

What can we do?

Would other energy sources help?

Which is the best energy source (oil / gas /
coal / wind / nuclear, solar or hydro-
electric power)?

Should cars be banned from city centres?

7

Situation:
Ms Burgham is the managing director of a big, international fast food group. The interviewer asks her some questions about environmental problems (What does the company do to avoid litter? Do they use plastic cups and bottles, or do they use materials which are biodegradable? What other things do they do for the environment?).

Listen to the interview and take notes. After that, discuss the interview in class or in small groups.

TORONTO HAS THE RIGHT STUFF

1
Discussion.

Have a look at the photos and the text on the opposite page.

Can you think of some changes in production methods and materials?

Which do you think are the most important? (Computers?
CAD / CIM?
Lean production?
Group work / team work?
New metals?
New plastics?
Robots?
Ceramic materials?)

Industrial welding robot at work

The crystalline structure of a memory alloy (magnified by 270:1).
The possibilities of using alloys which can "remember" their original form are being researched.

In the CAD / CAM sector life-long learning is an investment in the future.

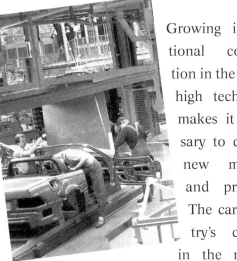

Growing international competition in the field of high technology makes it necessary to develop new methods and products. The car industry's chances in the marketplace will depend on how well they apply and utilize technologies that save energy and raw materials. Another important factor is the protection of health and environment. The Daimler-Benz company, for example, is working on experiments which involve powering vehicles by hydrogen drive. In cooperation with a number of Canadian and Norwegian institutions, they aim to convert hydroelectric energy into hydrogen, transport it to Germany via tankers, and then use it to power bus fleets, for instance.

Other ideas are also being discussed: solar roofs for motor vehicles, the use of memory metals and plastics, ceramic engines and fibre-reinforced carbons.

A LOOK AT GRAMMAR:

Modal auxiliaries with present perfect

When I switched the machine on, he was still working on it. –
    That might have been dangerous. (= I think it's possible that ...)

Yes, and I had a lot of trouble afterwards with my boss. –
    That must have been very unpleasant. (= I'm sure it was ...)

NOTE: The modal auxiliaries *must, can't, could, may* and *might* are often used to speculate about something in the past. Other examples: That can't have been very dangerous. / You could have lost your job. / That may have been a mistake.

2
Listen to the dialogue.

Driving back to London

a. Which advice would you give John and Mats? (Why?)

b. Have you ever been in a similar situation? If so, tell the other students about it.

LANGUAGE FUNCTIONS:

Compliments and thanks

Congratulations on your new product – it's a real innovation, I must say.

This *is* a very efficient lathe.

We do appreciate your help in this matter. – Don't mention it.

We'd like to express our thanks for your assistance. – Only too pleased to help.

Thank you for your help – it's really marvellous that you and your team got that engine repaired so quickly. – I was glad to be of service.

That's most kind of you.

3

Have another look at the "Language Functions" on the left. Choose the best answer from group "B" to the sentences in group "A":

A Merry Christmas!
 That's a very good report.
 Thanks a lot!
 Take the afternoon off.
 Would you like to come to the conference next Monday?

B I'm afraid I can't.
 That's most kind of you.
 Not at all.
 The same to you!
 Thank you.

4

Complete the sentences below by putting in a suitable preposition:

a. The new Lynx II bus is made … of some 1,700 parts and units which are all built to last.

b. Each component and each assembled part in the Lynx II is designed to work … the other for the smoothest running, most economic, easily maintained all round performance.

c. Only the best materials are used – the exhaust, for example, is made … stainless steel.

d. It takes years to design and develop a new bus such as the Lynx II – everything must be tested … make sure it meets the highest standards.

e. Many parts are manufactured … Leyland Bus, as, for instance, the gearbox – just one of the well tested and further developed components.

5

Situation:

You will hear descriptions of three different kinds of robots – independent robots, household robots, and industrial robots. Listen to the three texts and take notes.

(Which text belongs to which type of robot? Short description of the type of robot – what it is, what it can do, etc.).

INDUSTRIAL ROBOTS

Text number	Robot Description

INDEPENDENT ROBOTS

Text number	Robot Description

HOUSEHOLD ROBOTS

Text number	Robot Description

1

Read and listen. Before you listen to the recording, read the text on the opposite page and have a look at the drawing and the two photos below. Some words are missing, both in the drawing and in the text under the photos.

Now listen carefully to the recorded text and try to find the missing words (a to d):

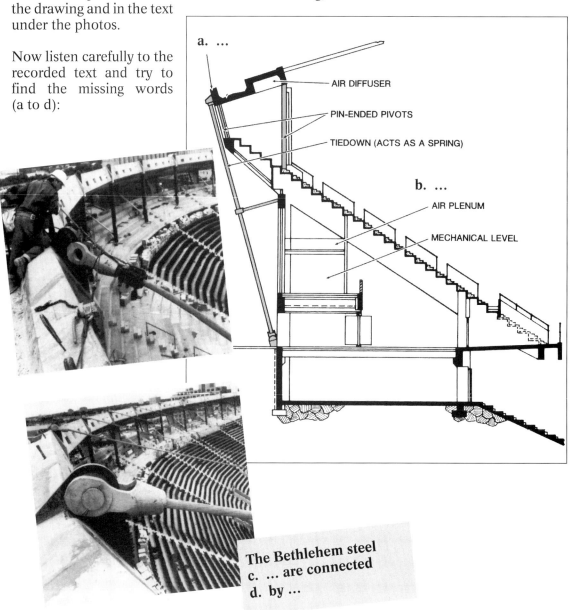

a. ...

AIR DIFFUSER

PIN-ENDED PIVOTS

TIEDOWN (ACTS AS A SPRING)

b. ...

AIR PLENUM

MECHANICAL LEVEL

The Bethlehem steel
c. ... are connected
d. by ...

The domed roof of the Hubert H. Humphrey Metrodome stadium in Minneapolis (Minnesota) consists of two layers of fabric reinforced by 166 tons of steel strand. The two layers create an air space that also provides thermal insulation. The roof allows enough light to pass through for day games yet reflects a large percentage of solar light and heat.

The main reason why costs for a cable-supported inflatable roof are lower than those for a fixed roof is the fabric structure's lighter weight and lower-cost materials. These, in turn, both simplify and speed construction and installation. In fact, the Metrodome's steel support cables took only 16 days to install. The entire stadium was completed for baseball on schedule – in just 27 months!

The steel cables that form the roof are $3\frac{3}{8}$-in.-diameter prestressed structural steel strand with the fabric attached to the strand by means of special clamps. This makes the roof look like a sea of inter-connected pillows. There are 18 main cables in the 166-ton support-system grid, nine in each diagonal direction.

The cables were installed by means of a crane and a winch. One by one, the crane lifted and joined the ends of each socketed strand to the steel-reinforced compression ring that goes around the top of the stadium.

According to the stadium architects, the roof is the largest ever built of double fabric. The airtight outer layer is $\frac{1}{32}$-in thick; the $9\frac{1}{2}$ acres of fabric were manufactured by Chemical Fabrics Corporation, North Bennington, Vermont.

Bethlehem Steel supplied 166 tons of $3\frac{3}{8}$-in.-diameter steel strand.

2

Use words from the warning signs below to complete sentences b, d and e:

LANGUAGE FUNCTIONS:

Opening conversations / Attracting people's attention Summarizing

a. On balance, I think we did the right thing.

b. To sum up, I think the … … should be kept free … and … .

c. Sorry to interrupt, but I think we should come back to the point you made earlier.

d. Talking of corrosion problems, I found a company that offers a good anti-corrosion paint for our … .

e. Well, actually, I think the … costs are too high.

3

Questions.

Where do you think can you find such a sign?

Why is it there?

What are you not allowed to do?

Why is it dangerous to be near a fork-lift truck?

What sort of accident do you think could happen?

A LOOK AT GRAMMAR:

"Each / Every", "One(s)", "All"

She knows each of them personally. (= of a limited number)
The tickets are $23 each.
They each have their own personal computer.

She asked me to check the machine every two days. (= not every day – today and not
   tomorrow, but again the day after tomorrow)
Every computer programmer was given a handbook. (= all the computer programmers)
He knows everyone in the company. (= every person)

The video they showed us was not a particularly good one.
"We've got them in blue and in red." – "Well, let's take a blue one, then."
Is this the one you mean?
These manuals are terrible – we need some new ones sooner or later.
"Which book do you want?" – "The one that's lying on the table."
This one's a bit small – have you got a slightly bigger one?
That's our chief engineer over there – he's the one who gives the orders.

All our machines are computer controlled. (= every machine)
He walked all the way to the station. (= the whole way to the station)
All our students passed the exam. (= everyone of our students …)

4
Talking to a car mechanic

Listening and note-taking. Listen to the dialogue and write down what's wrong with
John's car.

Pair work. Write a similar dialogue with another student.

5
Complete the sentences using "one" or "ones" and one of the following words:
better, clean, different, larger, new.

Example: These manuals are very old. We need …
       We need some new ones.

a. This handbook is too old. I must buy …

b. These tools are too dirty. I need …

c. This insulation isn't good enough. We need …

d. These toolboxes are too small. We should buy …

e. Why did you show them the video on cars? I think I would have shown them …

1

The text below and on the next page describes the gasification process. Have a look at the flowsheet on the opposite page and put the seven parts in the correct order. (On the recording you will hear the original text.)

The essential feature of the Babcock-IGI two-stage process is that coal is distilled in the first stage (distillation) producing a coke free of oil and tar for completely clean gasification in the second stage.

As this top gas is relatively cool, it is sent directly to a device which removes the tar. This tar is essentially free of water (below 1%), of good quality, and easily handled.

After the tar has been removed, the top gas passes into a cooler. After the cooling process, the top gas passes through a second device where the rest of the oil is taken out.

When the coal arrives, it is put into the distillation device where it goes down through gradually increasing temperature zones. All tar and other matter are removed until only coke remains.

Part of this clear gas is mixed with vapours from the distillation process and leaves the distillation chamber as "top gas" at a temperature of 100°–150°C.

In the gasification section, air and steam enter, and the carbon in the coke is completely gasified – apart from a small residue in the ash. The gas produced is free of oil and tar and known as "clear gas".

By this time, the clear gas has passed through a device in which dust is removed. The gas is then cooled to about 80°C before combining with the purified top gas to give a clean dust-free end product.

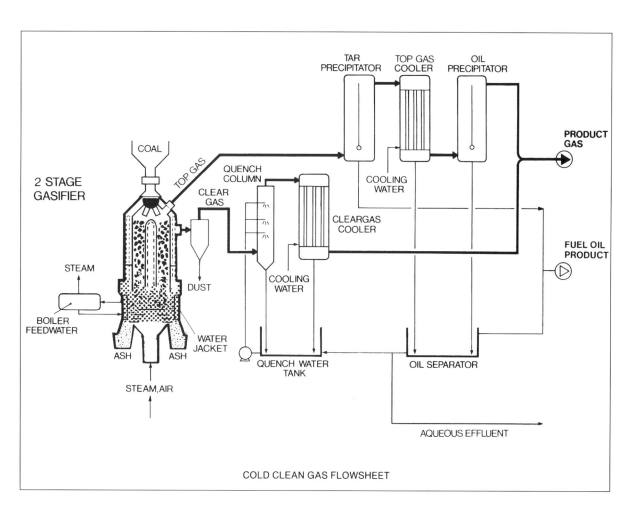

COLD CLEAN GAS FLOWSHEET

47

10

1
35

2

Have a look at the "Special features" on the opposite page (1. to 6.).
Which of these features is *not* mentioned in the short text on the recording?

Special Features

1. **High thermal efficiency**
2. **Gas easily treated to give sulphur free product if required**
3. **Easy start-up and shut-down**
4. **Simple clean-up operation**
5. **Automatic control to minimise staff**
6. **Complete elimination of many low-pressure coal gasification problems by Babcock-IGI unique two stage process**

3
Discussion.
This is the engineering concept of a typical fuel gas plant. What do you think about it? What is the best / worst place for such a plant? Discuss the environmental problems, if any.

"Have something done"

I'm going to *have* my car *repaired* tomorrow.
Have the machine *oiled*!
Last week I *had* the engine *checked*.
I must *have* my passport *stamped*.

NOTE: *Have something done* is used when you do not perform the action yourself but ask somebody else to do it: I can't repair a computer – I must have it repaired by an expert. Very often (particularly in spoken English) *get* is used instead of *have*: I'm going to get my car repaired tomorrow.
Compare these sentences:

Active: She's servicing her car. (= she's doing it herself)
Passive: Her car is being serviced. (= someone is doing it for her)
Causative: She's having her car serviced. (= she told / caused somebody to do it)

4
Answer as in the example:
I can't check the engine. → Well, you must have it checked by an expert.

a. I can't install the cable.

b. We can't clean the plant.

c. I can't program the new computer.

d. We can't oil the machine.

e. We can't test the new product here.

f. We can't repair the machine.

5
Answer as in the example:
My car is very dirty. → Why don't you have it washed, then?

a. The engine is not working. (check)

b. My car has a flat tyre and I can't repair it myself. (repair)

c. Our new brake system isn't working properly. (test again)

d. The machine is out of order. (check)

e. It's very difficult for us to install the new LAN network. (install)

6
Put in *all, every* or *one(s)*:

a. She translated ... the reports.

b. She had to call him ... other day.

c. There's a PC for ... engineer in the office.

d. I think they're ... going to the conference.

e. ... second motor must be replaced.

f. I'm sure ... day you'll be chief engineer.

g. I like apples but not the green ... .

8
Complete the following sentences by putting in the correct preposition:

LANGUAGE FUNCTIONS:

Apologies / invitations / offers

a. We do apologise ... this error. – Don't worry ... it.

b. I'm really sorry ... the delay. – Well, I suppose it couldn't be helped.

c. We were wondering if you'd like ... come ... our party next weekend. – Yes, I'd be delighted.

d. Would you like ... join us ... dinner? – That's most kind ... you.

e. Please accept our apologies ... the delay ... delivery. – It's perfectly all right – we received the spare parts just ... time.

7
A call from the company

Group work for three students. One of you is Ms Jones, one works in the reception of the Barkston Motel, and the third one is John.

Listen and take notes only for your special part.

Play the situation through.

9
Complete the following sentences by using the correct form of the words in brackets:

a. Up to three gasifiers can be ... by one ... operator plus one assistant. (control, lead)

b. It may ... preferable to ... a separate team of two or three daytime operators ... coal handling and general cleaning. (be, have, control)

c. The gasifier can be ... continuously if ... . (operate, require)

d. Coal transport and charging can be ... by the assistant operator. (control)

e. An electrician should ... available on a part time basis. (be)

A. Reading comprehension

Read the following passage through. There are numbered gaps in the text; choose the words from each group of words given on the right which complete the passage best.

When you eat an apple, you take in some of the energy that was taken from the sun by the apple tree. You can use that energy to lift a weight, ride a bicycle or push a lawn-mower. Your body is a sort of ... (1) which can do many things, but its power output is only a few hundred watts. Compare that to a small motor-mower, which has a power output of 2,000 watts. That's like having four or five people to push the mower for you while you ... (2) a walk round the garden!

Today, people in Britain use much more energy every day than they can get from their own bodies – at least 100 times more. A great deal of energy is used to power our cars, ... (3) our homes and run all our labour-saving machines. Factories use energy to make the things we use: as much energy goes into the making of one car as that car will use to go about 20,000 miles.

In Britain we ... (4) on energy for nearly everything we do. On average, each one of us uses about 30 times as much energy every day as a person in a developing country. Almost all our energy comes from coal, gas, oil or uranium. To make it useful we change it into different forms – like ... (5), which is a convenient way of bringing energy from a ... (6) into our homes.

1. a. engine
   b. lever
   c. pivot
   d. spring

2. a. has taken
   b. take
   c. takes
   d. taking

3. a. fill
   b. fire
   c. heat
   d. warm

4. a. depend
   b. go
   c. live
   d. work

5. a. batteries
   b. electricity
   c. LP gas
   d. modules

6. a. assembly plant
   b. factory
   c. filling station
   d. power station

B. Listening comprehension

You will hear four short texts with instructions and descriptions concerning a lamp. Listen to each text, then read the questions, then listen again and decide:

1. Text One belongs to picture

- A
- B
- C
- D

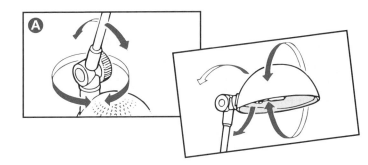

2. Text Two belongs to picture

- A
- B
- C
- D

3. Text Three belongs to picture

- A
- B
- C
- D

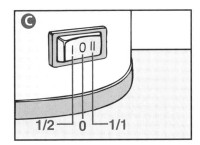

4. Text Four belongs to picture

- A
- B
- C
- D

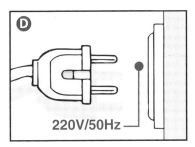

Testing

C. Can you match the explanations
   a to f to the pictures?

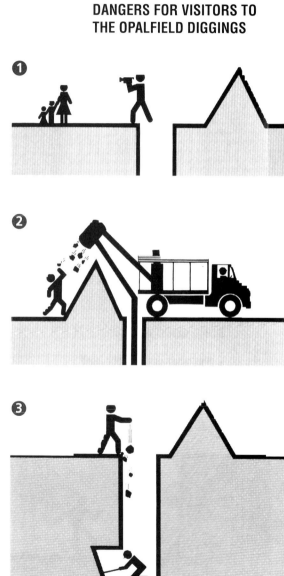

**DANGERS FOR VISITORS TO
THE OPALFIELD DIGGINGS**

❹

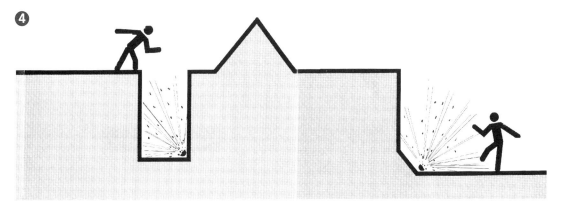

❺

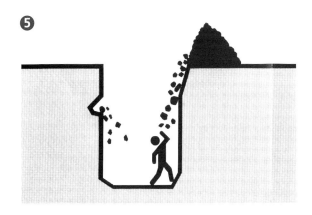

❻

a. **EXPLOSIVES**

Explosives are used extensively on working claims.

b. **OPEN MINE SHAFTS**

Thousands of shafts are scattered over the diggings, some up to 20 metres deep.

c. **DRIVING**

Miners' vehicles may be carrying explosives.
Tracks are narrow, rough, and winding. Many have blind corners and dangerous excavations nearby.

d. **ROCKFALLS**

Loose rocks on dumps or on the walls of open excavations can fall at any time.

e. **DANGER TO MINERS**

Thoughtless visitors can create dangers for miners.

f. **MACHINERY**

Mining machinery is very noisy and can be dangerous.
Operators may not notice your presence.

HOW PAPER IS MADE

1 FORESTS AND FELLING

Most paper is made from wood taken from the forests of Scandinavia, North America and some areas of Britain. These forests are carefully tended and for every tree that is felled for papermaking, two or three more are planted.

5 CLEANING

To remove all particles of dirt and lumps or pieces of tree bark, the pulp is thoroughly cleaned in water. It then goes into a vat to be bleached clean. Finally it is once more washed in water to remove the bleaching agents.

4 COOKING

The wood chips are cooked in massive pressure cookers with chemicals, water and steam which turn them into a kind of porridge called 'pulp.'

2 DEBARKING

Tree bark cannot be used to make paper so it is stripped from the logs. Nothing goes to waste, however, and the bark is burned as boiler fuel by the pulp mill.

3 CHIPPING

The stripped logs are fed through huge chipping machines which cut the wood into small pieces about 2 cms long.

7 **MIXING**

The refined pulp is poured into an enormous mixing vat to which hundreds of litres of water are added. To this mixture are added fillers, chemicals, size and dyes which will give the paper its final colour, strength and general appearance.

6 **REFINING**

Before the pulp can be made into a sheet of paper, the fibres have to be thoroughly beaten until they have broken to the correct length. It is also necessary to fibrillate (or fray the edges of) the fibres so that they will lock together to form the sheet of paper. This is done in a machine called a refiner.

To wet end of paper-machine

1

Read the explanations on this and the opposite page and look at the drawings.

On the recording, you will hear a conversation. Two members of an environmental group (Elaine and David) are talking with Robert, who works for the Canadian paper industry. They are talking about the logging industry – cutting trees, making timber for houses and industry, destroying the old growth ecosystem, and a lot of other questions and problems. Listen to the conversation, take notes, and discuss the arguments within groups or in the class.

A LOOK AT GRAMMAR:

Adjectives and adverbs (1)

Many adverbs are used to add to the meaning of a verb:

Adjective	Adverb
She is an *efficient engineer.*	She *works efficiently.*

However, adverbs can also be used to modify

- **adjectives:** It's *unpleasantly* hot in here, isn't it?
- **other adverbs:** She wrote the PC program *extremely quickly.*
- **prepositional phrases:** He's *completely* in the wrong, I'm afraid.
- **sentences:** *Personally,* I think he's a pretty good technician.

Adverbs are usually formed by adding "-ly" to an adjective: *careful – carefully, lucky – luckily.*

The adverb of "good" is "well": *She speaks English very well.*

Some words are used as adjectives and adverbs: *a fast car – she drives fast, an early train – she gets up early.*

Some adjectives can be used as adverbs with "-ly" or without "-ly", but there is a difference in meaning:

deep	She was deep in thought and didn't hear the phone ringing.
deeply	I'm deeply interested in electronics. (= *very / very much*)
hard	We all worked very hard to get the new machines ready on time.
hardly	I think he hardly noticed me. (= *almost not / very little*)
late	Because of a mechanical breakdown, the bus left half an hour late.
lately	Have you been to the cinema lately? (= *not long ago*)
near	Don't go too near – it could be dangerous!
nearly	That milling machine over there cost nearly $80,000. (= *almost*)

2

Listen to the dialogue and answer the following questions:

Can you go to Düsseldorf?

a. What's Simon working on at the moment?

b. Can anybody else take over? If yes, who?

c. What kind of new ideas do they expect to see at the exhibition?

3

Have another look at the "Language Functions" on the right and complete the sentences below by putting in *cause, damage, fault* or *pressure*:

a. Those tests are putting great … on the students.

b. The air … in this tyre is twenty pounds per square inch.

c. There is a … in the electrical system, I'm afraid.

d. What do you think was the … of the fire?

e. The accident did a lot of … to the forklift truck.

f. Did you see the accident last night? – Yes, as a matter of fact I did – and I'm quite sure it wasn't the driver's … .

g. The power failure was the … of the trouble.

h. At the moment, police are investigating the … of the explosion.

i. I'm not sure this was the … of the accident.

j. Whose … is this?

k. A … gauge is used for measuring fluid pressure.

l. I don't want to put … on you, but we haven't much time left.

LANGUAGE FUNCTIONS:

**Giving reasons
Cause and effect**

I'm sure this is the cause of the damage.

The damage was caused by an electrical fault.

The motor was installed with great care to keep it from interfering with the other machines.

The damage happened because of a fault in the power supply.

What made her do that?

The steam pressure makes the valve open.

Data transfer is effected by means of floppy discs.

We'll have to do something about that power failure. – All right, I'll have it seen to immediately.

4

The drawings on this page are in the correct order (1 to 9).
Can you find the text on the right which belongs to each drawing?
The texts are, of course, not in the correct order.
Can you make your own paper?

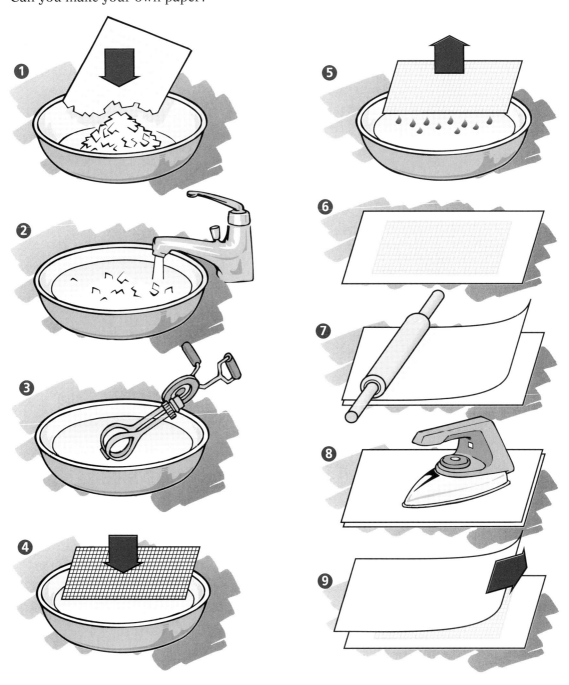

a. Fill the bowl with water (warm water is best). If you want to use starch, add two teaspoons to the water now.

b. Remove the blotting paper slowly, leaving your first sheet of hand made paper. This must be left for 24 hours to dry completely.

c. Tear the paper into very small pieces (not more than 1 inch square) and place in the bowl.

d. Cut a six-inch square of wire gauze (fine mesh). Dip the mesh into the bowl, then lift it up again flat.

e. Iron carefully until it is dry.

f. Let the paper soak for ten minutes, then beat it with the egg beater until it becomes mushy, with the fibres well dispersed.

g. Carefully remove the mesh and place the second sheet of blotting paper on top, and roll it firmly.

h. Turn the mesh upside down on to the blotting paper. This must be done carefully so that the pulp does not come apart.

i. Let the water drip back into the bowl.

1

Paper is used for a great variety of things.
Can you give examples?
When the first computers were introduced,
people said the "paperless office" would come.
Has this actually happened?
Discuss.

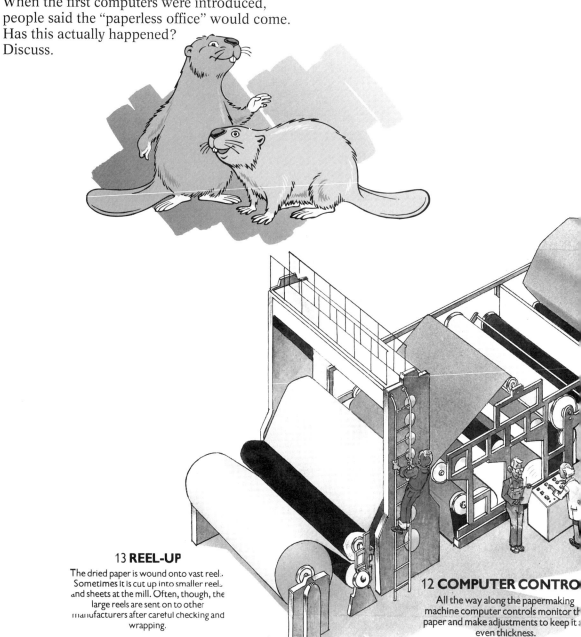

13 REEL-UP

The dried paper is wound onto vast reels.
Sometimes it is cut up into smaller reels
and sheets at the mill. Often, though, the
large reels are sent on to other
manufacturers after careful checking and
wrapping.

12 COMPUTER CONTRO

All the way along the papermaking
machine computer controls monitor th
paper and make adjustments to keep it a
even thickness.

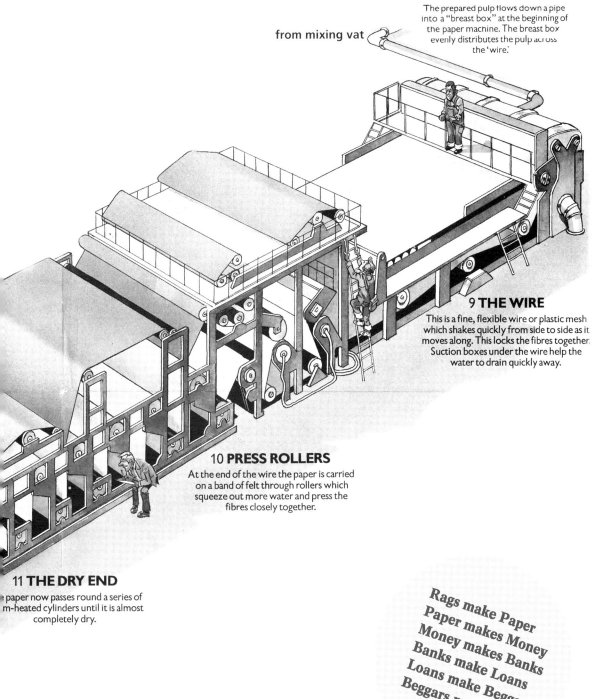

8 **THE WET END**

The prepared pulp flows down a pipe into a "breast box" at the beginning of the paper machine. The breast box evenly distributes the pulp across the 'wire.'

from mixing vat

9 **THE WIRE**

This is a fine, flexible wire or plastic mesh which shakes quickly from side to side as it moves along. This locks the fibres together. Suction boxes under the wire help the water to drain quickly away.

10 **PRESS ROLLERS**

At the end of the wire the paper is carried on a band of felt through rollers which squeeze out more water and press the fibres closely together.

11 **THE DRY END**

paper now passes round a series of m-heated cylinders until it is almost completely dry.

Rags make Paper
Paper makes Money
Money makes Banks
Banks make Loans
Loans make Beggars
Beggars make Rags

LANGUAGE FUNCTIONS:

Naming / defining / identifying

... and this is the Accounting Department.

This product is composed of plastic and steel.

The order consists of over 100 different items.

This device acts as a filter.

What we need for our plant is an efficient CAM system.

This switch, which is located at the rear, is designed to cut off the current in an emergency.

The machine standing over there is used for wrapping the parts in plastic.

The sensor mounted at the rear controls the thickness of the paper.

3

Read the text on the right (p. 65) and the "Language Functions" on the left carefully. Use these expressions to complete the sentences below:

- an efficient CAM system
- incineration of waste
- located at the rear
- to control the thickness
- to wrap the parts in plastic
- water quality protection

a. It's very important ... of plastic and steel.

b. I'm sure we will be able to reduce our operating costs by means of ... .

c. In order to protect them from pollution, they decided ... .

d. There are still a lot of cars on the road which have the engine ... .

e. ... is a complicated process which may pollute the air if it is not done properly.

f. In the last few years, paper mills have spent a lot of money on ... – as a result, some rivers and lakes are now much cleaner than they used to be.

2

Making travel arrangements

Listen to the dialogue and answer the following questions:

a. What is the reason for Simon's call?

b. Will Sue help him?

c. What does Simon promise Sue for her help?

"Environmental protection has been a national goal for many years … From the youngest students to senior citizens, nearly everybody is aware of the need to protect our environment …

In fact, Wisconsin's papermakers are among the national leaders in recycling, particularly in the use of recycled waste paper. The Wisconsin paper industry transforms millions of tons of waste paper into new, reusable products. Use of recycled waste paper in Wisconsin paper companies has grown enormously in the last few years. As a result, Wisconsin's recycling paper mills have always ranked first or second nationally in the use of recycled waste paper.

Another interesting point is water quality protection. Pulp and paper manufacturing requires large quantities of clean water. It is used – but not consumed – for cooking wood chips to create pulp, for washing and cleaning pulp, and in the actual papermaking process. Water may be used several times in the process before being cleaned and discharged, generally back into the source from which it was drawn.

The Wisconsin paper industry is also a leader in energy conservation. This is important because papermaking is energy-intensive – in fact, pulp and paper mills are the largest industrial energy users in Wisconsin. For our industry, energy conservation means the increased use of renewable energy sources. These sources include hydro-electric energy, plus the incineration of wood wastes, recycled automobile tires and bark … "

Wisconsin Paper Council

A LOOK AT GRAMMAR:

Adjectives and adverbs (2)

The position of adverbs

Some examples: They *frequently* clean the machine to avoid downtime.

They *obviously* don't know what we are talking about.
Obviously, they don't know what we are talking about.

She will *probably* take the eight o'clock plane to Birmingham.
We can *easily* solve this problem.

We would *certainly* have accepted their offer.
We *certainly* would have accepted their offer.

Unfortunately, they did not have any spare parts in stock.
They have *always* delivered the goods *punctually*.
I must say they pay their staff *very well* indeed.
After this, the machine *automatically* returns to the same cycle.

4

Where does the adverb go?

a. (eventually) – Friction causes a rolling ball to stop.
b. (freshly) – The walls were painted.
c. (frequently) – It rains in tropical forests.

d. (surprisingly) – It's easy to install this engine.
e. (carefully) – The bolt is inserted into the hole.
f. (extensively) – Explosives are used on working claims.

5

Listen to the following company announcement and answer the questions below.

Situation: In the past, pulp for the paper industry was usually bleached with chlorine or chlorine dioxide – both dangerous chemicals which can harm our environment. Nowadays, a lot of pulp mills produce unbleached pulp or use other methods for the bleaching process such as oxygen or hydrogen peroxide. Unbleached pulp is usually brown in colour and has impurities.

Now listen to the cassette and mark the sentences with   TRUE or FALSE:

a. The company they are talking about has a pulp mill in Vancouver.

b. The company's modernization and expansion programme will start next week.

c. The company will publish all the details of the new process next week.

d. For the bleaching process, the company will use oxygen and hydrogen peroxide.

Amazing science

- Look at this diagram of gears:

a. Write down the names of the things you would expect to have gears.

b. Write down the number of what you think is the best description of gears:

1. Wheels with teeth which transmit motion to wheels of a similar type.

2. Wheels which go round.

3. Wheels with teeth on them.

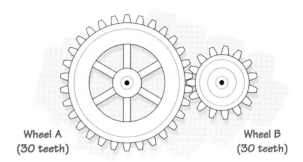

Wheel A
(30 teeth)

Wheel B
(30 teeth)

c. Look again at the diagram. Wheel A has 30 teeth, wheel B has 15. When the wheels turn together which of the following is true:

Wheel B will turn twice as fast as wheel A.
They will turn at the same speed.
Wheel A will turn twice as fast as wheel B.

- Look at these diagrams:

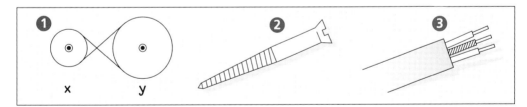

x   y

Now answer the following:

a. In diagram 1 if wheel X is turned in an anti-clockwise direction, in which direction does wheel Y turn?

b. When being put into wood is object 2 usually turned in a clockwise or anti-clockwise direction?

c. Copper wires c... electricity. What is the missing word?

1

Complete the following "Language Functions" by putting in the correct preposition:

LANGUAGE FUNCTIONS:

Explaining / showing the function

a. This report is ... the attention ... the Sales Department.

b. What's the point ... this?

c. It is not meant ... this machine.

d. This turbine was designed ... the new tanker.

e. What's the point ... checking the whole thing again?

f. He doesn't know anything ... steam trains.

g. It's bleached ... oxygen.

2

At Heathrow Airport

You will hear a conversation between Simon and an airport official. Work in groups and report to the class

a. how Simon gets to the departure level;

b. where the BA counter is.

3

Grammar revision:
Have another look at the grammar explanations of Unit 10 ("Have something done", p. 50). Answer the sentences below according to the following example:

Did she repair the motor-cycle herself? (by a garage mechanic last week) →
No, she had it repaired by a garage mechanic last week.

a. Do you always type the letters yourself? (by my secretary) ...

b. Are you going to paint the walls yourself? (by a professional painter) ...

c. Should I install this computer system myself? (by an expert) ...

d. Did she install the laser printer herself? (by Mr Miller) ...

e. Is she going to test the computer program herself? (by an experienced programmer) ...

f. Did he repair the drilling machine himself? (by our technician) ...

g. Shall I clean the electric motor myself? (by our service technician) ...

h. Did he translate the report himself? (by our export manager) ...

i. Are you going to design the turbines yourself? (by our design team) ...

j. Do you check the hardware yourself? (by a service technician) ...

k. Can I install the test equipment myself? (by a fitter) ...

①

4

Have a look at the four signs shown here. Then listen to the recording – you will hear some questions about each sign. Listen carefully, take notes and try to answer the questions.

③

②

④

13 A LOOK AT GRAMMAR:

Adjectives and adverbs (3)

In some cases, adjective and adverb have the same form and the same meaning …

Adjective	**Adverb**
I take a *daily* walk in the woods.	You must clean the machine *daily*.
Let's take the *early* train.	They set out *early* in the morning.
It's *easy* to ride a bike, isn't it?	Take it *easy*!
Fair play is very important in life.	The soccer team played very *fair*.
Barbara is a *fine* tennis player.	She did *fine* in the examination.
I'm glad to have a *free* afternoon today.	Children are admitted *free*.
That's a very *high* mountain.	Birds can fly very *high*.
He gets an *hourly* wage for his work.	The news is broadcast *hourly*.
He was the *last* person to leave.	John Hamilton arrived *last*.
The new assembly line is 130 m *long*.	Stay as *long* as you like.
The moon was *low* in the sky.	That airplane is flying very *low*!
An avenue is a *wide* street.	She has travelled far and *wide*.

… or the same form but a different meaning:

Adjective	**Adverb**
We polished the floor to make it *even*.	It was *even* worse than I thought.
His boss was a *just* man.	We've *just* run out of spare parts.
That's going to be our *only* chance.	*Only* three people survived the fire.
I hope this is the *right* tool.	Remember to turn *right*.
The bolt was *round* and about 5 cm long.	The wheel was spinning *round* and *round*.
I need a *sharp* knife for this job.	The meeting starts at six o'clock *sharp*.
He was *still* for a moment.	Sit *still*!
This is the *very* tool I want.	It's a *very* good transistor radio.

5

Put in a suitable preposition:

a. Common drawing standards are necessary to avoid confusion … industry.

b. Before I started the course, I didn't know a word … English.

c. Who is the inventor … the Möbius strip?

d. You're not allowed to smoke … here.

e. Let's have another look … the hardware – there must be something wrong.

The forests of the future?

A LOOK AT GRAMMAR:

Expressing the future

> I'll help you with the programming.
> I really hope she'll get the job.

will: relatively neutral form, often used after phrases like "I hope …", "I doubt …"

> Oh look! It's going to rain!
> They're going to be married soon.

going to: very common in speech, often (but not only) used for the "immediate" future

> We're spending next summer in Texas.
> She's arriving tomorrow morning at eight.

Present Progressive: used for events and activities planned for the future (usually with time adverbial)

> They will be arriving at any minute!
> When will you be seeing Mr Hart?

Future Progressive: polite form, often used for actions which will be in progress in the future

> The train to Hull leaves at six twenty.
> When does the next bus leave?

Simple Present: used for plans, arrangements etc. (e. g. train or bus schedules, timetables)

1

In this unit, you will see a lot of examples of the "future" as it is used in English (have a look at the grammar explanations on the left and the "Language Functions" below).

On the cassette/CD, you will hear a short text about Canada's forests and their future. Listen to the text and answer the following questions:

a. What do we find now in place of the tall trees?

b. Are people today responsible for changes to the forests? If so, why?

c. Can you answer the last two questions of the listening text? Write down your answer.

Compare your answers with the answers of the other students.

LANGUAGE FUNCTIONS:

Maintaining / ending a conversation

Am I making myself clear?
How do you mean?
What do you exactly mean by that?
Would you mind repeating that?
Could I ask you to say that again?
I don't quite see the point.
I'm not sure I understood you correctly.
Would you excuse me for a moment?
So, to sum up, we will …
I think that's about all there is to say.
I think we'll have to leave it there.
I think that's all, really.

2

A final briefing

Listen to the dialogue and answer the following questions:

a. Who made all the arrangements?

b. What kind of leaflet has Martina received?

c. Does it contain a lot of technical information?

d. What will Simon do if anything happens?

3

Group work. Read the text below and on the next pages, listen to it, and answer these questions:

a. What are the future changes people are talking about? Do you think they will happen?

b. What new machines might people use in future, according to the article?

c. Do you find the article more optimistic or more pessimistic? Give reasons.

Discuss your answers with the other students in the class.

Will forests look like orchards, with trees planted in straight rows? Perhaps radio-controlled robots will go up and down the rows, mowing the weeds, fertilizing the trees and spraying to control pests.

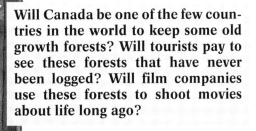

Will Canada be one of the few countries in the world to keep some old growth forests? Will tourists pay to see these forests that have never been logged? Will film companies use these forests to shoot movies about life long ago?

Will scientists find ways to make trees grow much faster? What other qualities might these "supertrees" have? Will people of the future grow trees that are free of knots, crooked sections or disease?

Will there be much less forest for logging than there is today? Will Canadians use up most of the old growth forests and then decide it costs too much to plant new forests? Will it be cheaper to buy wood from other countries than to grow and harvest our own?

How often have you thought, "There's got to be an easier way!" People are always looking for tools and machines that will help them do their work faster and better. It's the same in the forest industry. The industry hires scientists to develop new technology. This technology makes the industry more efficient and helps Canada compete with other countries that grow wood.

The early loggers who cut down trees with axes and huge handsaws would be amazed at today's computer-operated machinery. Today's loggers would probably be amazed at what forest technology will be like 50 years from now.

Will modern mills be completely run by computers and robots? Can you imagine a mill where logs go in one end, finished paper comes out the other end, and no workers are needed?

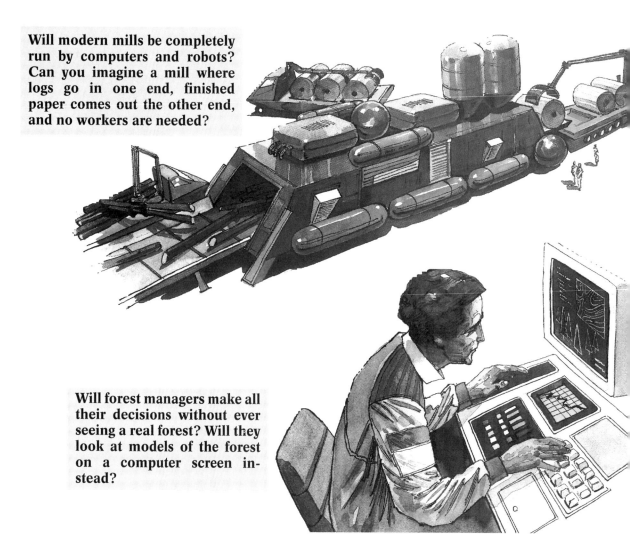

Will forest managers make all their decisions without ever seeing a real forest? Will they look at models of the forest on a computer screen instead?

Will forest companies use logging methods that do less damage to the environment? For instance, will loggers use huge balloons and other "lighter than air" machines to lift trees off steep hillsides?

Will there be a forestry retraining centre for workers whose jobs have been taken over by machines? Will robots do most of today's jobs in the forest while people do research and develop new technology?

We use different products today from the products people used in the past. A hundred years ago, school children did their work on slates, which are small blackboards. Today's students use paper. Future students may do most of their work on computer monitors. As consumers find new products that do a better job than the old ones, they switch.

People in the forest industry know this. They are always developing new products they think people will find useful. They are finding more and more uses for wood, especially waste wood. What products do you think people will be buying 50 years from now?

Will people of the future use different forest products from what we use today? Will they wear disposable paper clothing and eat high protein woodburgers?

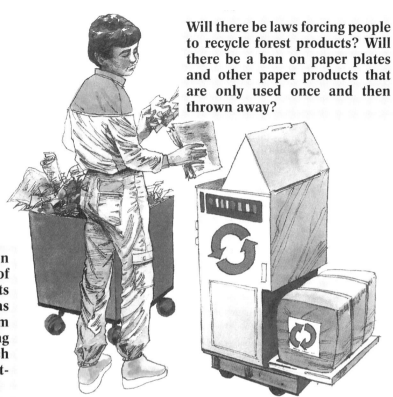

Will there be laws forcing people to recycle forest products? Will there be a ban on paper plates and other paper products that are only used once and then thrown away?

Will cars, jets and rockets run on fuel made from wood instead of gasoline? Will wood products replace other things, such as plastic, that are now made from oil? Will factories now running on hydro-electric power switch to power made by burning fast-growing wood?

Will people read newspapers on their home computer screens instead of on paper? Will Canada stop making newsprint?

1

Have a look at the drawing and the text on the opposite page. On the recording, you will hear another short text with some facts and figures.

With the information from the two texts and the drawing, you can find the missing parts below ("Building facts"):

Building facts

a. … reinforced concrete

b. Intermediate levels: … ft, … in.

c. Space between steel beams: … to … ft.

d. Total height of functional space and intermediate level: … ft, … in.

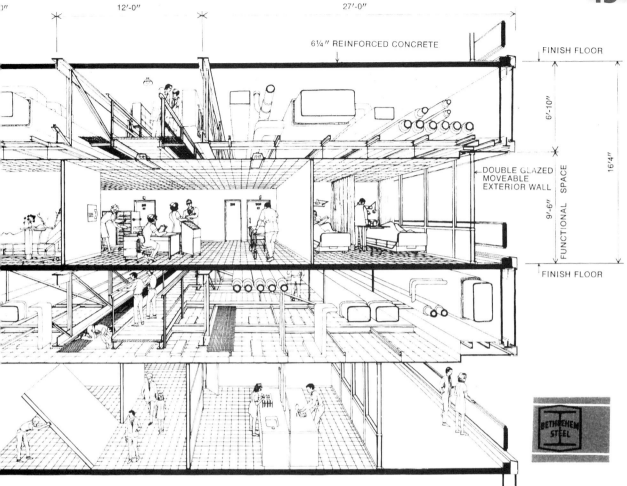

The new Los Angeles hospital provides the kind of flexibility that is necessary for modern medical technology. Design and planning studies resulted in a structure in the shape of a cross, built on a large two-storey base. A vertical shaft rises from the center of the base and houses the service and public elevator systems. Flexibility is further improved with intermediate levels located between each platform to house all the necessary mechanical and electrical systems. Each platform is independent from the other, and utilities are provided both through the ceiling and the floor. Air conditioning, plumbing and electrical services can be altered as required with minimum work.

A LOOK AT GRAMMAR:

Present perfect / Simple past

- The present perfect is often used to describe something which began in the past and is still continuing now. In such sentences, it combines past and present information and says how long this period of time has been:

Simple present: John is an engineer. He lives in Coventry and has got a VW Golf.

Simple past: John became an engineer in 1990. A year later, he moved to Coventry and bought a VW Golf.

Present perfect: John has been an engineer for many years. He has lived (or: has been living) in Coventry since 1990, and he has had a VW Golf since he moved there.

Other examples of the use of the present perfect:

- I haven't seen him for years.
- He hasn't written to me since Christmas.
- I've been here since Friday.
- Have you ever been to Canada?
- I have passed my driving test at last.
- Have you typed my report already?

- The simple past is used to talk about something which happened in the past and is now finished:

- His secretary phoned me a moment ago.
- Shakespeare was born in 1564.
- When did you write that letter?
- She played tennis every day when she was a girl.
- I passed my driving test last week.
- She arrived half an hour ago.

NOTE: It is very important to remember that in English the present perfect is not an alternative to the simple past. If a time adverbial is used (e. g. yesterday, last week, a minute ago), the simple past is the only correct form (not the present perfect!).

2

Complete the sentences below by putting in one of these words:

assured / forgot / informed / mentioned

LANGUAGE FUNCTIONS:

Reporting something to others

a. I … to him that the output figures were far too low.

b. She … me that she would deliver the spark plugs without delay.

c. He … to mention that he was going on holiday next week.

d. I was … of the problem by our agent in Stratford-upon-Avon.

e. Did you lock the workshop when you left the plant? – No, I'm afraid I … all about it.

f. At the last conference, the problem was hardly ever … .

3

Make sentences
Example: my brother / leave for work → My brother has just left for work.

a. John / clean the motor

b. the technician / repair the cylinder

c. Jack / test the solar panel

d. Mr Miller / make some phone calls

e. NASA / launch a satellite

f. I / talk to the computer programmer

g. our sales engineer / sell a turbine

h. Ms Lincoln / write the accident report

i. John / buy a CD player

4

Put in *ago, for* or *since*:

a. He's had his VW Golf … six years now.

b. She's been collecting stamps … she was fifteen.

c. I haven't seen her … we met in London several years … .

d. The world has been changing fast … the war.

e. He rang me up about three days … .

5

At Düsseldorf Airport

Listen carefully to the dialogue. With another student, write down a similar dialogue. You can use your own words, but if you remember expressions from the dialogue you heard, you can also use them.

16

Letterhead

34 Upper Fore Street
London N18 2SH
Tel.: 01-774 1856
Telex: 65344
Fax: 01-807 4303

References

Inside address

Pocknell & Co.
124 Rose Crescent
Luton, Beds LU1 5BH

Your ref: jp
Our ref: cm-k

Date
Also:
May 2, 19…
May 2nd, 19…
2nd May, 19…
5/2/19… (US)

2 May 19..

Attention line
Also:
For the attention of …

Attn: Joan Paddington

Dear Ms Paddington

Subject: Your request for cat brochure

Subject line

I have pleasure in enclosing a copy of the brochure in question. I do hope we will have the pleasure of welcoming you in our modern cat manufacturing plant.

Body of letter

Salutation
Dear Sir
Dear Sirs
Dear Sir or Madam
Dear Madam / Dear Sir
Dear Ms …
Dear Mr …
Gentlemen (US)

Yours sincerely

CHARLES MULLENDER

Charles Mullender
Sales Manager
KINDER TECH PLC

Complimentary close
Most common:
Yours sincerely (GB)
Sincerely (US)

Formal:
Yours faithfully (GB)

Encl

cc: Ms Deirde Ballin, Marketing

Carbon-copy notation

Enclosure
Also:
Enc(s)
Encl(s)

Addressing the envelope

- In modern business letters, addresses are usually written in block style (also called box style), i.e. all lines begin at the same point.

- Messrs is the plural of Mr and can be used when writing to a company whose name consists of two or more single names.

Abbreviations commonly used in the USA:

Alabama	AL	Indiana	IN	Nebraska	NE
Alaska	AK	Iowa	IA	Nevada	NV
Arizona	AZ	Kansas	KS	New Hampshire	NH
Arkansas	AR	Kentucky	KY	New Jersey	NJ
California	CA	Louisiana	LA	New Mexico	NM
Colorado	CO	Maine	ME	New York	NY
Connecticut	CT	Maryland	MD	North Carolina	NC
Delaware	DE	Massachusetts	MA	North Dakota	ND
Florida	FL	Michigan	MI	Ohio	OH
Georgia	GA	Minnesota	MN	Oklahoma	OK
Hawaii	HI	Mississippi	MS	Oregon	OR
Idaho	ID	Missouri	MO	Pennsylvania	PA
Illinois	IL	Montana	MT	Rhode Island	RI

South Carolina	SC
South Dakota	SD
Tennessee	TN
Texas	TX
Utah	UT
Vermont	VT
Virginia	VA
Washington	WA
West Virginia	WV
Wisconsin	WI
Wyoming	WY

(District of Columbia DC)

Messrs Hall & Burlington
PO Box 334
Leederville WA 6903
Australia

VIA AIR MAIL
CORREO AEREO

Mr Howard K. Donaldson
c/o Watson PLC
17 Palace Gate Road
Hampton Court, Surrey KT8 9BN
England

Air Mail Par Avion

Ms Joan Easton
American Chemical Corporation
23 East 56th Street
New York, NY 10022
USA

1

Read the text below. On the recording, you will hear a different text about catalytic converters and how they work – a short technical description.

In the drawings on the right and below, four items are missing (words and chemical formulas) – listen carefully and put the missing items in (you must find the chemical formulas yourself – on the recording, you will only hear the words):

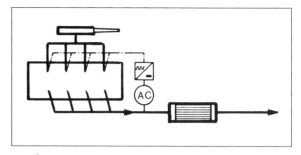

a. ... ...

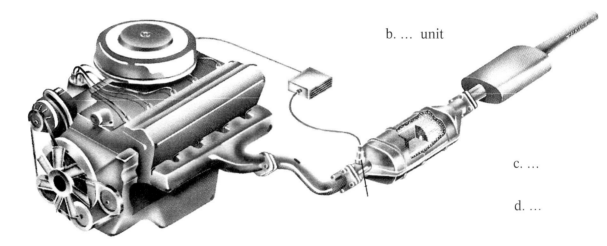

b. ... unit

c. ...

d. ...

The Catalytic Converter

Carbon monoxide and hydrocarbons can be converted into the harmless compounds carbon dioxide and water vapour simply through combustion with air. These compounds are already present in the air we breathe. It is also possible to remove nitrogen oxides by means of a reaction with carbon monoxide. Although these chemical reactions take place in the tailpipe, they do not occur quickly enough to remove enough pollutants from the car exhaust. There are materials, however, which cause the process to occur more quickly than if they were not present. Such materials are called catalysts – they do not take part in the reaction themselves. It is important to know that the engine must be operated with unleaded petrol. Otherwise, lead compounds in the exhaust would destroy the catalysts.

A LOOK AT GRAMMAR:

Passive (4)

Active	Passive
They discussed the tunnel project.	The tunnel project was discussed.
They built a new bridge.	A new bridge was built.
They used the fax machine.	The fax machine was used.
They cleaned all the tools.	All the tools were cleaned.
They replaced all the defective parts.	All the defective parts were replaced.

I wish I had been warned that the roads to Coventry were icy.

NOTE: Sometimes the agent is added with by:
The engineers made a proposal. – A proposal was made by the engineers.
They discussed the tunnel project. – The tunnel project was discussed by them.

Active: The technician gave him a new operating manual.
→ **Passive:** He was given a new operating manual (*by the technician*).

Active: They told her to check the oil level and the battery.
→ **Passive:** She was told to check the oil level and the battery.

Active: The salesman showed us the new digital satellite receivers.
→ **Passive:** We were shown the new digital satellite receivers (*by the salesman*).

Active: How much do they pay her a week?
→ **Passive:** How much is she paid a week?

Active: We must set up a completely new distribution system.
→ **Passive:** A completely new distribution system must be set up.

Discussing
a technical
problem ...

2

Listen to the dialogue and answer the questions below:

A drink at the hotel bar (1)

a. What is Simon interested in?

b. Does Jan's company still produce metal parts?

c. Which industry do they produce the parts for?

LANGUAGE FUNCTIONS:

Promising / offering to do something

The spare parts will be sent a.s.a.p.

The laser printers will be despatched today.

We promise to despatch the 500 switches within the next week.

May I be of assistance?

May I offer you my help?

If we can be of assistance, do not hesitate to contact us.

We can supply further parts on request.

Further supplies are available.

If you need more than the 20 bulbs we sent you, we can supply a further 15 within the next two months.

4

What must be done here? Make sentences with *must*:

a. Close this shutter at all times. – This shutter ... .

b. Remove helmets before entering. – Helmets ... .

c. In an emergency, pull handle and door. – In an emergency, handle and door ... .

d. If your ticket has a magnetic stripe, use the gates. – If ... .

e. Reduce speed now. – ... .

f. Extinguish all pilot lights. – ... .

g. Replace all protective covers after filling. – ... .

h. Read all the instructions carefully. – ... .

i. Discuss the problems with him. – ... .

3

Have a look at the grammar explanations of this unit (p. 85) and the sentences on the left. After that, change the sentences below into the passive form:

a. Ms Miller made all the phone calls to Canada.

b. The engineers discussed the technical problems this morning.

c. You have to replace all protective covers.

d. When will they install the new LAN network?

e. Uncontrolled gas flow can cause fire or explosion.

f. They will send you the manual under separate cover.

g. John will book the return flight tomorrow morning.

h. We can supply further parts on request.

i. We need 500 switches within the next two weeks.

5

Writing exercise

An American friend of yours has sent you a letter. In this letter, he tells you that in his country there are more and more foreign products nowadays. He wants to know from you what the situation in Germany is like. Write to him and tell him about

- cameras
- electronic equipment
- cars and lorries
- other technical products.

Use the correct form for letter and envelope.

1

Have a look at the photos below and the "Press Release" and answer these questions: What's Degussa's main activity? Does the company have plants in foreign countries? What sort of waste materials do they treat? What do they produce at the Rheinfelden plant?

Catalyst production at Degussa's plant in Rheinfelden

Press Release   Degussa

Precious-metal recycling for environmental protection

The recovery of precious metals is the most traditional area of activity for Degussa AG, Frankfurt, which was established in 1873 as the "German Gold and Silver Refinery". At that time, coins no longer in circulation and gold and silver items were the company's main source of material. Today, Degussa concentrates on the recovery of precious metals from industrial sources and from production waste.

Degussa recycles used materials and waste from the jewellery, electronics and electroplating industries as well as waste materials from the production of cutlery, mirrors and electronic components on a ceramic or plastic base, and catalysts from the chemical and oil refining industries. Large amounts of waste and residues from the film and photographic industry are also processed. And a completely new field is just beginning to open up: the recycling of used automotive exhaust catalysts. In Degussa's precious-metal recycling processes, many of the harmful materials connected with precious-metal waste are completely removed or destroyed.

MR FIX IT

IS ONLY A PHONE CALL AWAY

CALL 709 75 75

SUDBURY MOTOR INN
96 REGENT STREET SOUTH, SUDBURY, ONT P3E 3Z8

Please check the appropriate box and describe the problem and turn in at Front Desk.

- ❑ Television …
- ❑ Light Bulbs …
- ❑ Shower Head …
- ❑ Toilet …
- ❑ Plumbing …
- ❑ Door Locks …
- ❑ Air-Conditioning …
- ❑ Other …

Name …

Room number …

Date …

  2

Ms Lincoln is staying at the Sudbury Motor Inn. She is very angry because a lot of things in her room are out of order. She's calling Mr Fix It – listen to the dialogue and fill in the form accordingly.

After that, write a letter of complaint to the management. Tell them about all the trouble you had during your stay and ask for a refund.

PRIVATE ROAD
RESIDENT
PARKING ONLY
WHEEL CLAMPS
IN USE

3
Questions and discussion.

Look at the signs above.
What are you not allowed to do?
Why not?

What did the driver of the car below do?

Why do you think he / she parked in this place?

Do you think wheel
clamps are a good idea?
(Why? / Why not?)

What other methods are
there to control parking
in cities?

What do you think about
these methods?

A LOOK AT GRAMMAR:

"Some" and "any"

Some There are some letters for you on the table.
I've got some interesting newspapers for you.
There is someone (or: *somebody*) at the door.
She left something on the workbench over there.

Any We haven't got any operating manuals. (Or: *We've got no …*)
There isn't any oil in the tank. (Or: *There's no …*)
Any pen will do. (= *it doesn't matter which*)
There isn't anyone at the door.
She didn't leave anything on the table. (Or: *She left nothing …*)
Did he leave anything on the workbench?

NOTE: In negative sentences, *any* and *no* are used instead of *some*. When we expect (or hope to get) a positive answer, *some* may also be used in questions:
Have you got something by Agatha Christie? – Yes, of course.
Have you got some English newspapers for me? (= I know or I think you've got some – I expect the answer "yes")
Would you like some more coffee? (= polite question).

4

True or false? Listen carefully to the conversation and make a decision:

A drink at the hotel bar (2)

	TRUE	FALSE
a. At Eindhoven, they use plastic moulding equipment.	☐	☐
b. Jan thinks that using plastic moulding equipment might be a good idea.	☐	☐
c. At Eindhoven, they have some problems with tolerances.	☐	☐
d. At Simon's factory, they have to change sizes and measurements very often.	☐	☐
e. CAD/CAM controlled moulding processes cannot be used at the Eindhoven plant.	☐	☐
f. One problem is that the process they use at the Eindhoven plant is more expensive than other processes.	☐	☐

5

Have another look at the grammar of this unit (p. 90) and the "Language Functions" on the right. Complete the sentences below by putting in *any, no, not* or *some*:

a. In 1873, gold and silver items which were … longer fashionable were the company's main source of material.

b. … of the metal was used for refining.

c. It was … possible to use all the metal.

d. I know it was difficult but I hope I haven't caused … problems.

e. It's by … means cheap – in fact, it's quite expensive.

f. He's got a lot of books but he hasn't read … of them.

g. That's … what I wanted.

LANGUAGE FUNCTIONS:

Contradicting someone politely
Responding politely

Look, I don't think you can say that.

I don't really think so.

If I may say so, that's not quite the case.

I hope I'm not disturbing you. – By no means – come right in.

We hope we haven't caused any problems. – Not in the least.

I see your point but I'm afraid our company cannot be held responsible for mistakes other people made.

You must remember that you accepted responsibility for the installation of the parts.

6

Put in *about* or *through*:

a. She wrote an interesting book … recycling.

b. If you want to drive to Scotland, you'll have to drive … England.

c. Do you like driving … long tunnels?

d. That chip is … the size of a fingernail.

e. Water is pumped … this pipe at high pressure.

f. I don't like to drive straight … the centre of town.

g. The equipment they delivered last week weighs … two hundred kilograms.

h. A small motor-mower has an output of … 2,000 watts.

i. What was she complaining … ?

j. The guard at the entrance wouldn't let us … .

1

Listen to the four short texts on the recording (a to d). Which of these texts belongs to which headline (1 to 4 – see below on the right)?

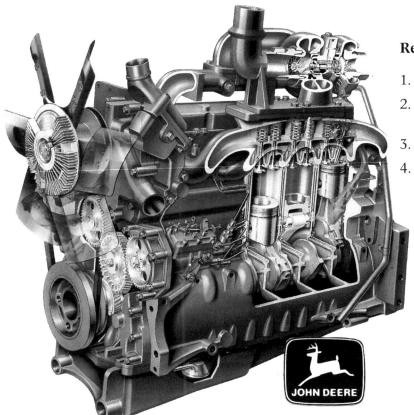

Reliable tractor engine

1. Low engine speed
2. High power over a wide range
3. Low piston speed
4. Piston spray cooling

JOHN DEERE

18

Complete the fax below by putting in *customers, engine, fuel* and *service*:

FAX MESSAGE

Ref. No: _____   Time Written: _1.30 pm_   Date: _1 / 3 / 19 .._

To: **Fax Number** _010 899602358_   Company: _JOHN DEERE SERVICE_   Attention: _TODD SUTTON_

From: **Fax Number** _0303 851113_   Company: _JOHN DEERE_   Originator: _JOHN MYERS_

Number of pages (inc. this page) (1)   For your information (✓)   Confirmation ( )   Please action ( )   Please reply on this fax ( )   Originator's Signature _____

MESSAGE:

> OPERATING MANUAL JOHN DEERE
> 3650 TRACTOR HAS BEEN MAILED TODAY.
>
> a. PLEASE TELL YOUR ... THAT A NEW
> b. ... CENTRE WILL BE OPENED
>   EITHER IN COLOGNE OR IN BONN – IT WILL
>   BE RESPONSIBLE FOR NORTH-RHINE
>   WESTPHALIA. AND DON'T FORGET TO MENTION
> c. OUR NEW ... WITH VERY LOW
> d. ... CONSUMPTION!
>
> BEST REGARDS
>
> *John Myers*
> MARKETING
> DEPARTMENT

3

Listen to the dialogue and answer these questions:

At the fair (1)

a. What does the company produce?

b. Where is it?

c. Is it a British company?

d. What does Ted Snyder do?

e. What is located in Hull?

Warning the tourists …
On a farm in Yorkshire, England:

DO NOT ATTEMPT TO
CROSS THIS FIELD
UNLESS YOU CAN DO IT
IN LESS THAN 9.9 SECS.
THE BULL CAN DO IT IN
10 SECS!

LANGUAGE FUNCTIONS:

Agreeing / admitting rejecting

We're in full agreement with their decision.

I fully accept what you say.

We can't approve of their decision – it will increase costs and cause delays.

I doubt very much whether they can deliver on time.

That has to be taken into account.

I take your point.

I must admit that I was counting on prompt delivery.

4

Put in *either*, *neither* or *nor*:

a. Which one shall I take? – It doesn't matter, you can take … .

b. We could find … the wrench … the screwdriver.

c. There are two roads that lead from here to the station. You can go … way.

d. I don't know … of these two men.

e. We didn't eat anything – … of us was very hungry.

18

"Either" / "neither" / "nor"
"Both"

Either   Either Ms Miller or her secretary is flying to London.
        She either speaks French, or she understands it. (= *I'm not sure*
           which is true)
        I can't repair a computer, either.
        Either of the motors would serve our purpose. (= *it doesn't matter*
           which of the two we use)
        Which do you like more? – I like either car. (= *I find the one as good*
           as the other)
        You can fit the appliance to either side of the machine. (= *it doesn't*
           matter which side you use)
        She doesn't like either of them very much.

Neither   Neither of them knew the answer. (= *none of the two ...*)
        I found two excellent motorbikes – the problem is that neither of them
           is cheap. (= *both are expensive*)

Nor   I had time for neither breakfast nor lunch today.
        He neither drinks nor smokes.
        He doesn't smoke, nor does he drink. (= *he doesn't drink, either*)

Both   We have two computers, but both of them are old. (= *not only the*
           one but also the other)
        I like these pocket calculators – I'll take both of them.
        She was a success both as an engineer and a manager. (= *she was*
           successful in both jobs)

Efficient power

You get almost full power, transmitted efficiently through one gear set. For light-duty work, you can shift up and reduce engine speed to conserve fuel even further.

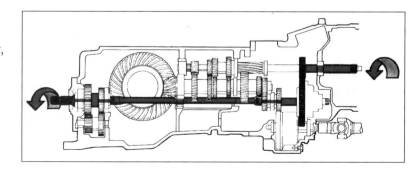

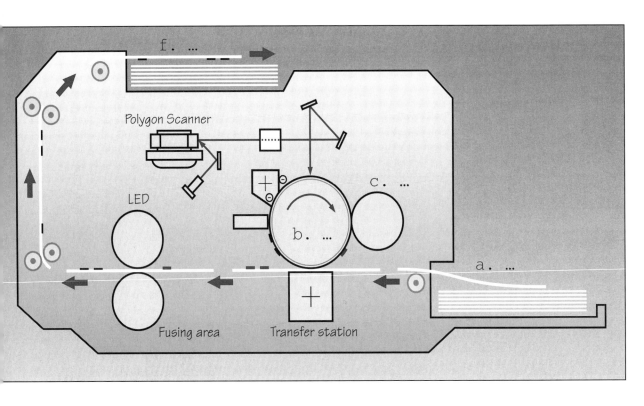

Polygon Scanner

LED

Fusing area   Transfer station

1
Listen to the recording and try to find the missing words in the drawings (a to f):

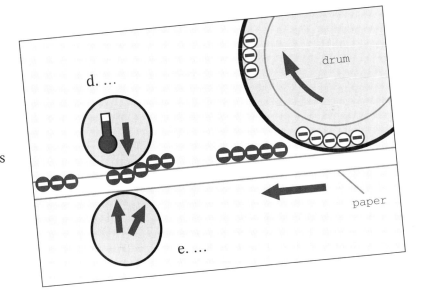

drum

paper

2

Complete the text below by putting in the following words:

class	memory
customer	requirements
features	sheet
interface	standard

With ten pages per minute, the MT911 sets a new ... (a) for mid-range printing ... (b). It makes no compromises in ... (c) expectations. As standard, it comes with a 200 ... (d) input cassette.

With the MT911, you buy a laser printer with all the right ... (e) and performance at an acceptable price.

Among the options, the MT911 offers you a serial ... (f), scalable fonts, and a 512 Kb ... (g). The MT911 has probably the lowest cost of ownership of any laser printer in its ... (h).

Agenda

Engineering Committee - Meeting to be held on Thursday, September 20, 19... at 10.15 at Head Office

1. Apologies for absence

2. Minutes of last meeting

3. Production report

4. Matters arising

5. Any other business

3

Complete the short minutes below by putting in the following verbs – be careful to use the correct form (for example *tell* or *told*):

come / decide / discuss / find / hold / receive / run / take / tell

When you have done that, answer the following questions:

- What sort of meeting was this?
- Where was it held?
- How many people were there? What are their jobs?
- What happened to the minutes of the previous meeting?
- What did Mr Roth say about production?
- Is the new model already on the market?
- When will the next meeting take place?

MINUTES

of the meeting of the Engineering Committee ... (a) on Thursday, September 20, 19... at Head Office

PRESENT: F Morgan (Chairperson)   S Tillett (Design Department)
         K Rothermere (Secretary)   C Upjohn (Sales and Marketing)
         L Roth (Chief Engineer)   A Sallingford (Purchasing)

1 APOLOGIES FOR ABSENCE: Were ... (b) from V de Vries (on business trip).

2 MINUTES OF THE LAST MEETING: The minutes of the previous meeting were ... (c) as read and adopted.

3 PRODUCTION REPORT: After a discussion of last week's problems, Mr Roth assured the committee members that production was now ... (d) at full capacity. There was still a slight problem with the delivery of components for the laser printers, but Ms Sallingford made it clear that a new supplier had been ... (e).

4 MATTERS ARISING: Ms Upjohn ... (f) the committee that a few questions had ... (g) up concerning the introduction of the new laser printer model. Mr Tillett pointed out that the final drawings would be on his desk in a day or two.
  It was ... (h) to ... (i) this point at the next meeting.

5 ANY OTHER BUSINESS: It was agreed to hold the next meeting at the same time and the same place a week from today.

DATE: CHAIRPERSON:

"So can I"

He can speak German. – So can I.
Mr Miller speaks English. – So do I.
She's interested in trains. – So am I.
She went to a meeting. – So did I.

I will buy a new pen. – So will I.
She should stop smoking. – So should I.
She's got a new car. – So have I.
I would do it. – So would I.

NOTE: In all the examples given above, the response *"Me too!"* is also possible, but it is very informal and cannot be used in all situations.

4

Listen to the dialogue – do not look at the text below. Listen again and try to make notes of what Simon is saying.

Imagine you are Simon – look at the text below and try to reconstruct what Simon is saying:

At the fair (2)

Jan:	Found a place where we can have lunch?
Simon:	…
Jan:	Oh no, a cafeteria will do.
Simon:	…
Jan:	Did you talk to that lady from Sweden?
Simon:	…
Jan:	Yes, I know. We're very satisfied with their machines and their service, I must say. Very reliable company.
Simon:	…
Jan:	Yes, it usually does at this time of day. There's a free table over there …

LANGUAGE FUNCTIONS:

Expressing regret, importance and belief

We regret to inform you that there will be a delay of about a week.

Unfortunately, we can't help you.

I was looking forward to seeing you at the fair.

It's essential that the parts arrive on time.

It's important that she should learn to use the DTP system.

Yes, I'm sure his advice would have been useful.

The goods certainly left here on time.

To err is human. To really foul things up requires a computer!

1

Listen to the recording and follow the instructions:

Text One: Are you good at arithmetic? Be prepared to double, add and divide. Get a pen or pencil and follow the instructions on the cassette.

Text Two: There are lots of hidden numbers in a word. In "*to*night", for example, you can actually hear a "two". The text you are going to hear is full of such numbers. Listen to the sentences and write down all the numbers you can hear.

LANGUAGE FUNCTIONS:

Expressing uncertainty and concern

I'm not at all certain whether this was the right decision.

That might be true, but I'd like to make sure first.

I must say I'm not very much in favour of this proposal.

We are very concerned about the low quality of the washers.

We do hope that they will get the machine repaired by tomorrow.

May I express the hope that our business contacts will continue?

I can't help wondering if these plastic parts will really do the job.

2

Have a look at the "Language Functions" on the left. Choose words from those sentences to fill the gaps:

a. The good thing is that these … … do not need any lubrication.

b. I really hope you will … your car repaired by next week.

c. I'm not at all … whether it is correct to lubricate this machine with grease.

d. … are small disks of metal, fibre, rubber, or plastic used to make something watertight, such as a water tap, for instance.

e. She showed me an interesting … for a new shopping centre in the middle of Stratford-upon-Avon.

8	1	6
3	5	7
4	9	2

Here is a magic square

It is magic because the sum of each row, each column and each diagonal is the same.

Let us check to see that this is true:

Rows: 8 + 1 + 6 = 15
         3 + 5 + 7 = 15
         4 + 9 + 2 = 15

Diagonals: 8 + 5 + 2 = 15
            4 + 5 + 6 = 15

Columns:
```
        8       1       6
        3       5       7
        4       9       2
       ___     ___     ___
       15      15      15
```

15 is called the MAGIC CONSTANT.

The square contains other patterns. See if you can find them.
Here is a start: 4, 5, 6 (diagonal).

(The others are 3, 5, 7; 2, 5, 8; 1, 5, 9. Note that these sequences are made by adding 1, 2, 3 and 4 respectively.)

There is a formula for calculating the magic constant. If the magic square is 3 x 3, then n in the formula is 3; if the square is 4 x 4, then n is 4 and so on.

Here is the formula:

Magic Constant $= \dfrac{n}{2}(n^2 + 1)$

Thus, for a 3 x 3 square: MC $= \dfrac{3}{2}(3^2 + 1)$

$\qquad\qquad\qquad = \dfrac{3}{2} \times 10 = 15$

(The formula assumes that the numbers used are 1 to 9 for 3 x 3 and 1 to 16 for 4 x 4; i. e. not ANY numbers.)

Here is a 3 x 3 magic square with some of the numbers missing. See if you can complete the square.

		6
	5	
4	3	

4 + 5 + 6 = 15, so the magic constant is 15.
Check this, using the formula again:

$\dfrac{n}{2}(n^2 + 1) = \dfrac{3}{2}(9 + 1)$

$\qquad\qquad\qquad = 3 \times 5 = 15$

This is a very famous magic square

16	3	2	13
5	10	11	8
9	6	7	12
4	15	14	1

It was made up by a German artist called Albrecht Dürer in 1514.
Can you see the date in the square?
Use the formula to find the magic constant

$\dfrac{n}{2}(n^2 + 1) = \dfrac{4}{2}(16 + 1)$

$\qquad\qquad\qquad = 2 \times 17 = 34$

Check   (a) the rows
         (b) the columns
         (c) the diagonals

What is the sum of the four corner squares? (34)
What is the sum of the four central squares? (34)
What is the sum of the numbers in each quarter square, i. e. the 2 x 2 squares which make up the large square? (34)

20

Useful phrases for telephone calls

33

Hello, switchboard, can I have a line, please?

Operator! I'd like to make a long-distance call to San Francisco, please.

Hold on a moment! I have an urgent trunk call for you.

Who's speaking, please?

Hello. Is that Mr Jones? – Yes, speaking.

Hold the line, please.

Hang on a minute, please.

I'm calling long-distance. Please connect me with the sales
   department.

I'll put you through.

Could you ask her to ring me back?

I'm afraid he's engaged just now.

Sorry, the line is busy.

Sorry, wrong number.

I'd like to speak to John Hayling, please.
   I think it's extension 228.

Is this a collect call, sir?

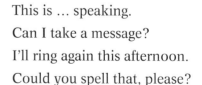

This is … speaking.

Can I take a message?

I'll ring again this afternoon.

Could you spell that, please?

Could you repeat that slowly, please?

3

Writing a short report in memo form.

Situation:
Mr Tillett visited the CNC Fair in Brisbane to get some more information on the competitors' machines. He sent a report to his Chief Engineer, Mr Roth.

The report is shown below – but there are some lines missing.

Complete the report with the sentence parts below (a to h):

    attached you will find
    can be programmed off-line
    can be used for production
    I had a very close look
    in our machines, too
    the company you mentioned
    the main features include
    we discuss this matter

Working at the machining centre

MEMORANDUM

FROM *Stephen Tillett*

TO *Lenny Roth*

DATE *24 / October / 19 . .*

SUBJECT: CNC Fair, Brisbane

… (a) (Boxhill) has a stand with some very interesting designs on display. … (b) at their Vertical Machining Centre 260MC – really up to date.

The 260MC … (c) as well as for training purposes – an important selling point. … (d) CNC programming with full colour tool-path graphics, VDU, data library.

The machine … (e) and interfaced to CAD/CAM. It can also be linked to full robotic FMS/CIM packages. I think we should consider something like that … (f)

… (g) their sales literature – I strongly suggest that … (h) at our next Engineering Committee meeting in November.

RICHMOND ENGINEERING COMPANY • BOWMANS COTTAGE • WINDSOR NSW 2369

4

Listen to the following dialogue and fill in the missing information below:

Making a phone call

a. The weather in Düsseldorf is … .

b. The weather in Manchester is … .

c. Simon got information on …

and on … .

d. Jan put Simon into contact with a Swedish company which has … .

e. The phone number is … .

5

You are taking part in an international conference. You have to introduce yourself. Include the following points:
Your name / Your nationality / Your job / Your company / Which languages you speak / The hotel you are staying at.

Somebody starts smoking. Ask politely to restrict smoking on the conference. Suggest a break from time to time instead.

You think it's time for a coffee break. Suggest this.

A foreign company representative asks you about one of your company's new products. You are not familiar with the technical details. What do you say?

You have beeen having an interesting conversation with another conference participant and would like to continue the discussion to clear up all the important questions. Unfortunately, however, you are due at a meeting in a couple of minutes. What do you say?

You see that somebody you know has parked his or her car under a no-parking sign. What do you say?

A LOOK AT GRAMMAR:

"Neither/nor can I"

He can't speak German. – Neither can I.
I wasn't in Stratford-upon-Avon last summer. – Neither was I.
She isn't interested in the development of tractors. – Neither am I.
I won't buy a new pen. – Neither will I.
She didn't go to that meeting yesterday. – Neither did I.
She shouldn't eat so much sugar. – Neither should I.
I wouldn't tell him about the mistake in the program. – Neither would I.
She doesn't like American cars. – Neither do I.

NOTE: In all the sentences shown above, *neither* may be replaced by *nor*. *Me neither* and *Nor me* are also possible responses, but they are very informal and cannot be used in all situations.

6

Answer with "So ..." or "Neither ...":

a. I know her very well.

b. I wouldn't buy that old car.

c. She usually drives too fast.

d. I can't read his handwriting.

e. She wasn't in Wales last year.

f. He collects stamps.

g. I won't go to France next year.

h. I can't play the piano.

i. I was in London last week.

j. She went home early.

k. I haven't seen him.

l. She can write computer programs.

m. I couldn't do that.

n. She lives in a big city.

o. I wasn't informed.

p. She wrote a lot of letters.

q. He fell asleep.

A. Reading comprehension

Read the text and answer the questions on the right according to the information given in the text by marking a, b, c or d:

Degussa Catalysts for Automotive Emission Control

Many years ago, the Degussa AG started producing automotive exhaust gas catalysts in its Rheinfelden plant for European manufacturers exporting cars to the United States and Japan.

Growing motorisation has produced a sharp increase in air pollution (mainly carbon monoxide, hydrocarbons and nitrogen oxides) in many countries. As a result, the USA, Japan and the European Union developed plans at the end of the sixties to solve this problem. Since the beginning of the seventies, limits on the pollutant contents of automobile exhaust gas have been introduced.

In the course of these developments, it became clear that this problem could not be solved by modifications of engine combustion processes alone. Of all possible solutions, the use of catalytic converters in the USA and Japan proved to be the most efficient. Since its first application in the USA, this method has become widely accepted. Millions of passenger cars throughout the world are now equipped with catalytic exhaust emission converters.

The catalysts, which generally consist of ceramic materials coated with platinum or similar metals, are installed in the car's exhaust system. In combination with other measures such as fuel/air mixture control, the catalytic converters eliminate a large part of the pollutants in the exhaust emission.

For the purification of diesel exhaust gas, Degussa has developed a different system which reduces the ignition temperature.

1. The Degussa Rheinfelden plant

    a. exports exhaust gas catalysts to the USA.
    b. has been operating for many years.
    c. produces export cars.
    d. started operation this year.

2. According to the text, the increase in air pollution comes from

    a. an increase in the number of cars.
    b. bigger engines.
    c. more exhaust gas from the same number of cars.
    d. more US cars.

3. Modifying the engines used in our cars

    a. proved to be the most efficient answer to our problems.
    b. was required by law.
    c. was tried in the USA and Japan.
    d. will not solve the pollution problem.

4. Many catalysts

    a. are coated with ceramic materials.
    b. are used in combination with bigger engines.
    c. consist of ceramic materials coated with metals.
    d. do not work with fuel/air mixture control.

5. The catalysts Degussa has developed

    a. can be used for petrol and diesel engines.
    b. eliminate a large proportion of the pollutants in the exhaust emission.
    c. eliminate all pollutants in the exhaust emission.
    d. eliminate platinum.

B. Listening comprehension

You will hear seven short texts.
Listen to the text, then read the sentences below. Take three minutes for this.
After that, listen to the text again. Now mark whether the sentences are TRUE
or FALSE (one, two or three sentences can be TRUE):

TEXT ONE   **Computer game for children**   TRUE   FALSE
  6. The manufacturer of the game is not mentioned in the text.
  7. The new computer game is for children aged between five and seven.
  8. With this game, children can learn basic mathematics.

TEXT TWO   **"Green" engine reduces pollution**
  9. Saab has built a new factory for this engine.
 10. The engine's cat has taken five years to develop.
 11. The new engine was introduced in Frankfurt.

TEXT THREE   **Electric water purifier**
 12. The appliance does not work if there are bacteria in the water.
 13. The purifier has a capacity of more than five litres.
 14. The water purifier was developed in Australia.

TEXT FOUR   **Lightweight portable printer**
 15. The printer is made by a company in England.
 16. The printer runs on AC or batteries.
 17. The printer weighs less than two kilograms.

TEXT FIVE   **Hovercraft for all surfaces**
 18. Handling the "SCAT 46" is easy.
 19. The "SCAT 46" can be used on ice and snow.
 20. Up to six people can sit in the "SCAT 46".

TEXT SIX   **International Summer Electronics Show**
 21. At this show, you can meet people from 1,400 cities.
 22. Computers will not be shown.
 23. The visitors to this show come from more than 80 countries.

TEXT SEVEN   **Corrosion a big problem?**
 24. Metal parts more than three metres wide cannot be coated.
 25. The new anti-corrosion coating protects metal surfaces.
 26. The PlastiComp Corporation makes pipes and fittings.

... *and finally: A Science Fiction Story*

THE FUN THEY HAD

Isaac Asimov

Margie even wrote about it that night in her diary. On the page headed 17 May, 2155, she wrote, 'Today Tommy found a real book!'

It was a very old book. Margie's grandfather once said that when he was a little boy *his* grandfather told him that there was a time when all stories were printed on paper.

They turned the pages, which were yellow and crinkly, and it was awfully funny to read words that stood still instead of moving the way they were supposed to – on a screen, you know. And then, when they turned back to the page before, it had the same words on it that it had had when they read it the first time.

'Gee,' said Tommy, 'what a waste. When you are through with the book, you just throw it away, I guess. Our television screen must have had a million books on it and it's good for plenty more. I wouldn't throw *it* away.'

'Same with mine,' said Margie. She was eleven and hadn't seen as many telebooks as Tommy had. He was thirteen.

She said, 'Where did you find it?'

'In my house.' He pointed without looking, because he was busy reading. 'In the attic.'

'What's it about?'

'School.'

Margie was scornful. 'School? What's there to write about school? I hate school.' Margie always hated school, but now she hated it more than ever. The mechanical teacher had been giving her test after test in geography and she had been doing worse and worse until her mother had shaken her head sorrowfully and sent for the County Inspector.

He was a round little man with a red face and a whole box of tools with dials and wires. He smiled at her and gave her an apple, then took the teacher apart. Margie had hoped he wouldn't know how to put it together again, but he knew how all right and after an hour or so, there it was again, large and black and ugly with a big screen on which all the lessons were shown and the questions were asked. That wasn't so bad. The part she hated most was the slot where she had to put homework and test papers. She always had to write them out in a punch code they made her learn when she was six years old, and the mechanical teacher calculated the mark in no time.

The inspector had smiled after he was finished and patted her head. He said to her mother, 'It's not the little girl's fault, Mrs Jones. I think the geography sector was geared a little too quick. Those things happen sometimes. I've slowed it up to an average ten-year level. Actually, the overall pattern of her progress is quite satisfactory.' And he patted Margie's head again. Margie was disappointed. She had been hoping they would take the teacher away altogether. They had once taken Tommy's teacher away for nearly a month because the history sector had blanked out completely.

So she said to Tommy, 'Why would anyone write about school?'

Tommy looked at her with very superior eyes. 'Because it's not our kind of school, stupid. This is the old kind of school that they had hundreds and hundreds of years ago.' He added loftily, pronouncing the word carefully, '*Centuries* ago.'

Margie was hurt. 'Well, I don't know what kind of school they had all that time ago.' She read the book over his shoulder for a while, then said, 'Anyway, they had a teacher.'

'Sure they had a teacher, but it wasn't a *regular* teacher. It was a man.'

'A man? How could a man be a teacher?'

'Well, he just told the boys and girls things and gave them homework and asked them questions.'

'A man isn't smart enough.'

'Sure he is. My father knows as much as my teacher.'

'He can't. A man can't know as much as a teacher.'

'He knows almost as much I betcha.'

Margie wasn't prepared to dispute that. She said, 'I wouldn't want a strange man in my house to teach me.'

Tommy screamed with laughter, 'You don't know much, Margie. The teachers didn't live in the house. They had a special building and all the kids went there.'

'And all the kids learned the same thing?'

'Sure, if they were the same age.'

'But my mother says a teacher had to be adjusted to fit the mind of each boy and girl it teaches and that each kid has to be taught differently.'

'Just the same they didn't do it that way then. If you don't like it, you don't have to read the book.'

'I didn't say I didn't like it,' Margie said quickly. She wanted to read about those funny schools.

They weren't even half finished when Margie's mother called, 'Margie! School!'

Margie looked up. 'Not yet, mamma.'

'Now,' said Mrs Jones. 'And it's probably time for Tommy, too.'

Margie said to Tommy, 'Can I read the book some more with you after school?'

'Maybe,' he said, nonchalantly. He walked away whistling, the dusty old book tucked beneath his arm.

Margie went into the schoolroom. It was right next to her bedroom, and the mechanical teacher was on and waiting for her. It was always on at the same time every day except Saturday and Sunday, because her mother said little girls learned better if they learned at regular hours.

The screen was lit up, and it said, 'Today's arithmetic lesson is on the addition of proper fractions. Please insert yesterday's homework in the proper slot.'

Margie did so with a sigh. She was thinking about the old schools they had when her grandfather's grandfather was a little boy. All the kids from the whole neighbourhood came, laughing and shouting in the school-yard, sitting together in the school-room, going home together at the end of the day. They learned the same things so they could help one another on the homework and talk about it.

And the teachers were people …

The mechanical teacher was flashing on the screen: 'When we add the fractions 1/2 and 1/4 –'

Margie was thinking about how the kids must have loved it in the old days. She was thinking about the fun they had.

Isaac Asimov (1920-1993): US biochemist and writer, born in Russia, known particularly for his science-fiction stories and novels; his family emigrated to the USA in 1923, and he became an American citizen in 1928; he grew up in Brooklyn and was educated at Columbia University, New York; Isaac Asimov began writing science-fiction stories in 1939; his many books include *I, Robot*, *The Caves of Steel*, and *The Foundation Trilogy*; after 1958, he worked mainly on scientific textbooks for schools and universities and works of popular science; in 1979, he became professor of biochemistry at the University of Boston.

Isaac Asimov is also well-known for his famous "Three Laws of Robotics", which try to make it clear what must be programmed into an "intelligent" robot to make it safe for human beings:

1. A robot may not injure a human being, or, through inaction, allow a human being to come to harm.
2. A robot must obey the orders given it by human beings except where such orders would conflict with the First Law.
3. A robot must protect its own existence as long as such protection does not conflict with the First or Second Law.

Questions on the text

1. Why were Margie and Tommy so surprised about the book Tommy found?
   What was so different?
2. Why did Tommy think these old books were a waste?
3. Why was Margie scornful when she heard that the old book was about school?
   What did she say about her school?
4. Why had her mother sent for the County Inspector?
5. What happened after about an hour when he had repaired everything?
6. Which part did Margie hate most?
7. What had happened with the geography sector and what did the County Inspector do about it?
8. Why was Margie disappointed?
   What had once happened with Tommy's teacher?
9. Describe the kind of school children had long ago.
10. What did Margie think about those old schools and the teachers at that time?
11. What had her mother said to her about teachers?

Group work and discussion

Do you think that in future teachers will be replaced by robots?
What are the advantages or disadvantages?

1. Divide the class into two groups.
2. One group speaks about the advantages, the other group about the disadvantages. Each group writes down their arguments.
3. General discussion (after about 15 minutes). Each group tries to convince the members of the other group.
4. The group which was able to convince most members of the other group is the winning team.

Discussion

List all the duties of the mechanical teacher and compare them to the job of a human teacher.
What do you think about Margie's and Tommy's school?
Do you think this school is nicer than the schools with a human teacher? Give reasons for your answer.
What did children like Margie miss most with the mechanical teacher?

For vocabulary see page 159.

A technical dictionary – words and phrases

GB = der Ausdruck kommt hauptsächlich im britischen Englisch vor
US = der Ausdruck kommt hauptsächlich im amerikanischen Englisch vor
A = Arbeitsbuch
T = Test

Die Zahlen verweisen auf die Lektionen, in denen der Ausdruck in einer bestimmten Bedeutung zum ersten Mal vorkommt.

A

abbreviation [əbriːvɪ'eɪʃn] 16 Abkürzung
ability [ə'bɪlətɪ] 7 Fähigkeit
absence ['æbsəns] 19 Abwesenheit; *apologies for absence* ... entschuldigt fehlen...
access ['ækses] A2 Zugang; Zugriff; *access for delivery* Zufahrt für Lieferanten
accidentally [æksɪ'dentəlɪ] 2 zufällig; versehentlich
according [ə'kɔːdɪŋ] 3 *act according to the rules* sich an die Regeln halten; *according to her opinion* ihrer Meinung nach; *react accordingly* entsprechend reagieren
account [ə'kaʊnt] 12/18 *take something into account* etwas in Betracht ziehen
accounting department [ə'kaʊntɪŋ] 12 Buchführung(sabteilung)
acid ['æsɪd] 4 Säure; *acid rain* saurer Regen
across [ə'krɒs] 3/12 *one third of the way across* auf ein Drittel Breite; *across the wire* quer über den Draht
act [ækt] 9/12 *it acts as a spring* es fungiert als Feder
action ['ækʃn] A12 Handeln; Aktion; Maßnahme(n)
active ['æktɪv] A17 aktiv; wirksam
activity [æk'tɪvətɪ] 6/7 Tätigkeit; Aktivität; *area of activity* Einsatzbereich; Tätigkeitsbereich
actual ['æktʃʊəl] 9/12/13/16 *the actual papermaking process* der eigentliche Papierherstellungsprozeß; *well, actually...* nun, eigentlich... *has this actually happened?* ist das tatsächlich passiert?
add [æd] 3/11 hinzufügen; addieren
additional [ə'dɪʃənl] 18 zusätzlich
address [ə'dres] 2 adressieren; anreden; Adresse
adjoining [ə'dʒɔɪnɪŋ] 3 *adjoining parts* nebeneinanderliegende Teile
adjustment [ə'dʒʌstmənt] 12 Justierung; Anpassung; Regulierung; *some adjustments are necessary on your engine* bei Ihrem Motor muß einiges neu eingestellt werden
admit [əd'mɪt] 18 zugeben
adopt [ə'dɒpt] 19 *the minutes were adopted* das Protokoll wurde angenommen
adult ['ædʌlt/ə'dʌlt] T2 Erwachsene(r)
adventure [əd'ventʃə] T2 Abenteuer
advice [əd'vaɪs] 16 *can you give me some advice?* können Sie mir einen Rat geben?
aerial ['eərɪəl] 12 Antenne
aeroplane → airplane
aerosol can ['eərəʊsɒl] 7 (*auch:* spray can) Sprühdose
affect [ə'fekt] 14 sich auswirken auf; *rust has affected the spark plugs* Rost hat die Zündkerzen in Mitleidenschaft gezogen
agent ['eɪdʒənt] 3/11/15 *bleaching agents* Bleichmittel; *the local agent* der örtliche Vertreter
agreeable [ə'grɪəbl] 10 angenehm

agreement [ə'gri:mənt] 18 Zustimmung; Übereinstimmung; *we're in full agreement with their decision* wir stimmen voll mit ihrer Entscheidung überein

agriculture ['ægrɪkʌltʃə] 13 Landwirtschaft

ahead [ə'hed] 8/13/16 *looks like some heavy traffic ahead* da vorne scheint ziemlich viel Verkehr zu sein; *ahead of the actual catalyst* vor dem eigentlichen Katalysator

aim [eɪm] 8 *they aim to convert hydro-electric energy into hydrogen* sie zielen darauf hinaus, hydroelektrische Energie in Wasserstoff umzuwandeln

air-diffuser ['eə dɪ'fju:zə] 9 Luftverteiler

air plenum ['eə 'pli:nəm] 9 Luftkammer

air pollution ['eə pə'lu:ʃn] T2 Luftverschmutzung

air-supported ['eə sə'pɔːtɪd] 9 luftgestützt (= *pneumatische Konstruktion*)

aircraft ['eəkrɑːft] 13 Flugzeug(e)

airline ['eəlaɪn] 13 Fluggesellschaft

airplane ['eəpleɪn] *(GB auch:)* aeroplane ['eərəpleɪn] 3 Flugzeug

alloy ['ælɔɪ] 8 Legierung

alphabetic [ælfə'betɪk] A1 alphabetisch

alter ['ɔːltə] 15 (ver)ändern

alternative [ɔːl'tɜːnətɪv] 5 alternativ

aluminium [æljʊ'mɪnɪəm] *(US:)* aluminum [ə'lu:mɪnəm] 1 Aluminium

amaze [ə'meɪz] 4/13 *they would be amazed* sie wären verblüfft; *amazing* erstaunlich, verblüffend

analogue ['ænəlɒg] A19 analog; Analog-

angle ['æŋgl] 3/11 Winkel; *a right angle* ein rechter Winkel

announce [ə'naʊns] 12 bekanntgeben; durchsagen

anti-clockwise ['æntɪ'klɒkwaɪz] 1/13 gegen den Uhrzeigersinn

anti-corrosion ['æntɪkə'rəʊʒn] T2 Rostschutz-; Korrosionsschutz-

apart [ə'pɑːt] 10/11 *apart from* abgesehen von; *come apart* auseinandergehen; auseinanderfallen; *take something apart* etwas auseinandernehmen

apologize [ə'pɒlədʒaɪz] 10 sich entschuldigen

apology [ə'pɒlədʒɪ] A10 Entschuldigung

appliance [ə'plaɪəns] 18/A2 Gerät

application [æplɪ'keɪʃn] T2 *(hier:)* Anwendung; *(auch:)* Bewerbung

apply [ə'plaɪ] 8/17 anwenden; *the applied process* das angewandte Verfahren

appreciate [ə'pri:ʃɪeɪt] 8/16 *we do appreciate your help* wir sind Ihnen für Ihre Hilfe wirklich dankbar

apprentice [ə'prentɪs] 1 Auszubildende(r)

appropriate [ə'prəʊprɪət] 2/17 passend; geeignet

approve [ə'pru:v] 18 *we can't approve of their decision* wir können mit ihrer Entscheidung nicht einverstanden sein

approximate [ə'prɒksɪmət] A8 ungefähr

aqueous effluent ['eɪkwɪəs 'eflʊənt] 10 wässerige Emission(en)

architect ['ɑːkɪtekt] 9 Architekt

arise [ə'raɪz] (arose [ə'rəʊz] – have arisen [ə'rɪzn]) 19 auftauchen; aufkommen; *matters arising (etwa:)* zusätzliche Tagungsordnungspunkte

artificial [ɑːtɪ'fɪʃl] 5 künstlich

ash [æʃ] 10 Asche

aspect ['æspekt] A3 Gesichtspunkt; Aspekt

assembly [ə'semblɪ] A1/8/9 Zusammenbau; Montage; Versammlung; *steel strand assemblies* Stahlseilmontageteile; *assembly line* Montageband, Fließband

assist [ə'sɪst] 17 helfen; assistieren

assistance [ə'sɪstəns] 8/16/19 Hilfe; *may I be of assistance?* kann ich helfen? *professional assistance* fachmännische Hilfe

assume [ə'sju:m] 16/20 vermuten; annehmen; *the formula assumes that...* die Formel geht davon aus, daß...

assumption [ə'sʌmpʃn] 6 Vermutung; Annahme

assure [ə'ʃʊə] 15/19 versichern; *he assured me that...* er versicherte mir, daß...

astronaut ['æstrənɔːt] 4 Astronaut(in)

astronomer [ə'strɒnəmə] 3 Astronom(in)

atmosphere ['ætməsfɪə] 7 Atmosphäre; Luft

atom ['ætəm] A5 Atom

attach [ə'tætʃ] 6/9 befestigen; verbinden; *attached to the strand* verbunden mit dem Seil

attachment [ə'tætʃmənt] T2 Zusatzgerät; Zusatzvorrichtung

attack [ə'tæk] 7 Angriff; angreifen

attempt [ə'tempt] 18 versuchen; *make an attempt* einen Versuch unternehmen

attend [ə'tend] 6 besuchen; teilnehmen (an); *attend a business meeting* an einer geschäftlichen Besprechung teilnehmen; *attend a university* eine Universität besuchen

attention [ə'tenʃn] 9/13/16 *attention Ms Brown* zu Händen von Ms Brown; *pay attention* passen Sie auf! *for the attention of…* zu Händen (von/des)…; *pay attention to environmental problems* Umweltproblemen Aufmerksamkeit schenken; *attract attention* Aufmerksamkeit erregen

attraction [ə'trækʃn] 13 Anziehung; Anziehungskraft

attractive [ə'træktɪv] A3 anziehend; attraktiv

automatic [ɔːtə'mætɪk] 10 automatisch

automobile ['ɔːtəməʊbiːl] 8 *(US:)* Auto

automotive [ɔːtə'məʊtɪv] 1/17 *automotive engineer* Automobilbauingenieur; *automotive exhaust catalysts* Katalysatoren für Autoabgase

average ['ævərɪdʒ] 7/T1 *the average family* die Durchschnittsfamilie; *on average* im Durchschnitt

aware [ə'weə] 12 *I wasn't aware of this* ich war mir dessen nicht bewußt

axe [æks] 14 Axt

axle ['æksl] A8 Achse

B

back and forth ['bæk ənd 'fɔːθ] A5 hin und her; vor und zurück

background ['bækgraʊnd] Hintergrund

bacteria [bæk'tɪərɪə] *(Einzahl:* bacterium [bæk'tɪərɪəm]) A11/T2 Bakterien

balance ['bæləns] 9 Gleichgewicht; Schwebe; *on balance* alles in allem

balloon [bə'luːn] A13 Ballon

ban [bæn] 7/14 Verbot; verbieten; *a ban on paper plates* ein Verbot von Papiertellern

band [bænd] 3/12 Band; Streifen

bar [bɑː] 6 Stange

bark [bɑːk] 11 Rinde *(eines Baumes)*

base [beɪs] 15/17/T2 Basis; Grundlage; Fundament; basieren (auf); *on a plastic base* auf Kunststoffbasis; *base vehicle* Basisfahrzeug

basic ['beɪsɪk] 16/T2 *basic mathematics* Mathematikgrundlagen; *have a basic knowledge* Grundkenntnisse haben

bath [bɑːθ] 17 *electroplating bath* Galvanisierbad

battery ['bætərɪ] 4 Batterie

beam [biːm] 4/A5 Strahl; Balken; Träger; (aus)strahlen; *steel beam* Stahlträger; *beam up to a satellite* zu einem Satelliten schikken; *it's beamed back down to earth* es wird auf die Erde zurückgestrahlt

beggar ['begə] 12 Bettler

behalf [bɪ'hɑːf] 5 *on behalf of…* im Namen von…

bench grinder ['bentʃ 'graɪndə] 1 Tischschleifmaschine

bend [bend] 1/A13 biegen; knicken; *does it bend?* biegt es sich?

beware [bɪ'weə] 9 Vorsicht!

bicycle ['baɪsɪkl] T1 Fahrrad

billion ['bɪljən] *(US:)* Milliarde *(wird in zunehmendem Maße so auch in Großbritannien verwendet)*

biodegradable [baɪəʊdɪ'greɪdəbl] 7 biologisch abbaubar

bit [bɪt] 1 Stück; Teil; *screwdriver bits* Schraubeinsätze

blackboard ['blækbɔːd] A14 Tafel *(= Schultafel)*

bleach [bliːtʃ] 11 Bleichmittel; bleichen; *bleach clean* sauber bleichen; *unbleached* ungebleicht

blind corner [blaɪnd] T1 unübersichtliche Ecke

blotting paper ['blɒtɪŋ] 11 Löschpapier

board [bɔːd] 11/A19 Karton (= *Pappe)*; Brett

boiler [ˈbɔɪlə] 10 Kessel; *boiler feedwater* Speisewasser für den Kessel

bolt [bəʊlt] 1/3 Schraube; Bolzen; Durchsteckschraube; *door bolt* Türriegel

bore [bɔː] 5 Bohrung; bohren; aufbohren

borrow [ˈbɒrəʊ] 2 leihen; borgen

bowl [bəʊl] 11 Schüssel; Schale

brake [breɪk] 9/10 Bremse; bremsen; *brake system* Bremssystem

brand-new [brænd'njuː] 16 brandneu

break [breɪk] 6 Pause

breakdown [ˈbreɪkdaʊn] 11 Panne; *a breakdown in the system* ein Zusammenbruch des Systems

breast box [ˈbrest bɒks] 12 *(Papierherstellung:)* Stoffauflauf *(= Kasten mit Zellstoffbrei)*

brickwork [ˈbrɪkwɜːk] 10 Mauerwerk

brief [briːf] A3/14 *brief somebody* jemand (kurz) unterrichten (= informieren); *a brief explanation* eine kurze Erklärung; *briefs* Instruktionen; *briefing* Briefing *(= kurze Unterrichtung; Einsatzbesprechung)*

brightness [ˈbraɪtnɪs] T1 Helligkeit

broad [brɔːd] 12 breit

broadcast [ˈbrɔːdkɑːst] 4 Sendung

building site [ˈbɪldɪŋ saɪt] 5 Baustelle

bulb → light bulb

bull [bʊl] 18 Stier, Bulle

burglar [ˈbɜːglə] 16 Einbrecher

burner [ˈbɜːnə] 16 Brenner

by [baɪ] 8/9/11/A11/12 *by means of* mittels; *magnified by 270:1* zweihundertsiebzigfach vergrößert; *one by one* einer nach dem andern; *what do you mean by that?* was meinen Sie damit?; *reduce emissions by more than 80%* die Emissionen um mehr als 80% verringern

C

cable [ˈkeɪbl] 6/9 Kabel; *cable-supported* von Kabeln gehalten

calculate [ˈkælkjʊleɪt] A19/20 berechnen; ausrechnen; errechnen

can [kæn] 7/12 *aerosol can* Sprühdose; *garbage can* Mülleimer

candle [ˈkændl] A13 Kerze

candy bar [ˈkændɪ ˈbɑː] 12 *(etwa:)* Schokoladenriegel

cap [kæp] 2 Kappe; Haube; Verschluß

capacity [kəˈpæsətɪ] 2 Leistung; Leistungsfähigkeit; Kapazität; *the machine is working to capacity* die Maschine ist voll ausgelastet

carbon [ˈkɑːbən] A9 Kohlenstoff

carbon dioxide [ˈkɑːbən daɪˈɒksaɪd] 16 Kohlendioxid

carbon monoxide [ˈkɑːbən mɒˈnɒksaɪd] 16 Kohlenmonoxid

cardboard boxes [ˈkɑːdbɔːd ˈbɒksɪz] 12 Kartons

care [keə] 14 *with great care* mit großer Sorgfalt

carton [ˈkɑːtən] 12 Karton

case [keɪs] 5/16/17 Fall; *in that case…* in diesem Fall …; *case history* Vorgeschichte; *in case of emergency* im Notfall; *that's not quite the case* das ist nicht ganz so

cast-iron [ˈkɑːstˈaɪən] 1 Gußeisen

CAT → catalytic converter

catalogue [ˈkætəlɒg] 1 Katalog

catalyst [ˈkætəlɪst] 16 *three-way catalyst* Dreiwegekatalysator

catalytic converter [kætəˈlɪtɪk kənˈvɜːtə] T2 Katalysator

cause [kɔːz] A7 Ursache; verursachen

ceiling [ˈsiːlɪŋ] 15 Decke *(Zimmerdecke)*

cell [sel] 15 Zelle; *solar cell* Solarzelle

Centigrade [ˈsentɪgreɪd] 4 Celsius

centre punch [ˈsentə pʌntʃ] 1 Körner

ceramic [sɪˈræmɪk/kɪˈræmɪk] 8/17 keramisch; *on a ceramic basis* auf keramischer Basis

channel [ˈtʃænl] 5/10 Kanal; *the English Channel* der Ärmelkanal

charge [tʃɑːdʒ] 18/19/20/T2 *she's in charge of sales* sie leitet den Verkauf; *electric charge* elektrische Ladung; *charge a battery* eine Batterie aufladen; *a new charge* eine neue Charge *(= Ladung)*

chassis [ˈʃæsɪ] A8 Fahrgestell; Chassis

check [tʃek] 2 Prüfung; prüfen

cheque [tʃek] 1 Scheck (*US:* check)

chemical ['kemɪkl] 1/4/A12/16 *chemical engineer* Chemieingenieur; *chemical pulp* Chemiepulpe, Vollzellstoff; *chemical corporation* Chemiekonzern; *chemicals* Chemikalien

chief [tʃiːf] 7/A10/15 Haupt-; *chief engineer* Chefingenieur; *chiefly* hauptsächlich

chips [tʃɪps] 11/12 Splitter; Schnitzel; Chips; *wood chips* Holzschnitzel; *potato chips* Kartoffelchips

chipping machine ['tʃɪpɪŋ] 11 Häckselmaschine

chlorine ['klɔːriːn] 12 Chlor

chlorine dioxide ['klɔːriːn daɪ'ɒksaɪd] 12 Chlordioxid

circle ['sɜːkl] 3 Kreis; kreisen, umkreisen

circuit ['sɜːkɪt] 15 Schaltung; Stromkreis

circulation [sɜːkjʊ'leɪʃn] 17 Kreislauf; Zirkulation; *in circulation* im Umlauf

civil engineer ['sɪvl] 1 Bauingenieur(in)

clamp [klæmp] 9/17 Klammer; Zwinge; *wheel clamp* Parkkralle

classify ['klæsɪfaɪ] A19 einteilen; klassifizieren

clean [kliːn] 7/10 *clean up the environment* die Umwelt säubern; *a simple clean-up operation* ein einfacher Säuberungsvorgang

clear [klɪə] 14 *clear land* Land urbar machen

clear gas ['klɪəgæs] 10 Klargas

climate ['klaɪmɪt] 7 Klima

climb [klaɪm] 5 klettern

clockwise ['klɒkwaɪz] 13 im Uhrzeigersinn

close [kləʊs] 4/12 *it will bring us closer* es wird uns näher bringen; *get close enough* nahe genug herankommen; *closely together* nahe beieinander

close [kləʊz] 2/4/15/16 *the valve must be closed* das Ventil muß geschlossen werden; *close this matter* die Sache abschließen; *the circuit can be closed* der Stromkreis kann geschlossen werden

clothing ['kləʊðɪŋ] 14 Kleidung

clutch [klʌtʃ] A18 Kupplung

coal [kəʊl] 7/16 Kohle; *coal mine* Kohlenbergwerk

coat [kəʊt] 1/A17/T2 *you can coat these parts* diese Teile können beschichtet werden; *coated with platinum* mit Platin beschichtet; *a coat of paint* eine Farbschicht

coke [kəʊk] 10 Koks

colleague ['kɒliːg] 6 Kollege/Kollegin

collect [kə'lekt] 20 *collect call* R-Gespräch

colon ['kəʊlən] 16 Doppelpunkt

column ['kɒləm] 10/20 Säule; Pfeiler; Kolumne

combination [kɒmbɪ'neɪʃn] A12 Verbindung; Kombination

combine [kəm'baɪn] 10 verbinden; kombinieren

combustion [kəm'bʌstʃən] 12/T2 Verbrennung

come [kʌm] 11/14 *the points which come up* die Punkte, die auftauchen; *come apart* auseinandergehen

commerce ['kɒmɜːs] 3 Handel

commercial [kə'mɜːʃl] A1 kaufmännisch; Handels-; kommerziell

committee [kə'mɪtɪ] 19/20 Ausschuß; Komitee

communication [kəmjuːnɪ'keɪʃn] 4/11 Kommunikation; *communications satellite* Nachrichtensatellit

compare [kəm'peə] 10/18 vergleichen

compartment [kəm'pɑːtmənt] 2 Fach; Abteil(ung)

compass ['kʌmpəs] A16 Kompaß

compatible [kəm'pætəbl] T2 kompatibel

compensation [kɒmpen'seɪʃn] 12 Ausgleich; Ersatz; Kompensation

compete [kəm'piːt] 14 *compete with other countries* mit anderen Ländern im Wettbewerb stehen

competition [kɒmpɪ'tɪʃn] 8 Konkurrenz; Wettbewerb; *be in competition with somebody* mit jemandem konkurrieren

competitor [kəm'petɪtə] 20 Konkurrent

complain [kəm'pleɪn] 1 sich beschweren

complaint [kəm'pleɪnt] 6 Beschwerde; *make a complaint* eine Beschwerde vorbringen

complete [kəm'pliːt] 1/9/10/16/17/20 vollständig; völlig; vervollständigen; *completely new* ganz neu; *completely gasified* völlig in Gas verwandelt; *a completely new field* ein völlig neuer Bereich

complicated ['kɒmplɪkeɪtɪd] 5 kompliziert

compliments ['kɒmplɪmənts] 8 Komplimente

complimentary close [kɒmplɪ'mentərɪ] 16 höflicher Abschluß *(eines Briefes)*

comply [kəm'plaɪ] A13 sich nach etwas richten; mit etwas übereinstimmen; *comply with the regulations* die Bestimmungen einhalten

component [kəm'pəʊnənt] 17 Teil

compose [kəm'pəʊz] 12 *it is composed of…* es besteht aus…

composition [kɒmpə'zɪʃn] 16 Zusammensetzung; Mischung

comprehension [kɒmprɪ'henʃn] T1 Verstehen; Verständnis

compression ring [kəm'preʃn] 9 Kompressionsring

concentrate ['kɒnsəntreɪt] 4/17 (sich) konzentrieren

concept ['kɒnsept] 9/10/15 Konzept; Idee; Vorstellung

concern [kən'sɜːn] 2/T1/20 *as far as the LP gas system is concerned* was das LP-Gassystem angeht; *we are very concerned about the low quality* wir machen uns große Sorgen über die schlechte Qualität; *facts concerning a lamp* Tatsachen, die eine Lampe betreffen

concrete ['kɒnkriːt] 15 Beton

conduct [kən'dʌkt] 12 *conduct a test* einen Test durchführen

confusing [kən'fjuːzɪŋ] 13 verwirrend

congratulations! [kəngrætjʊ'leɪʃnz] 8 herzlichen Glückwunsch!

conservation [kɒnsə'veɪʃn] 12 Erhaltung; Konservierung; *energy conservation (etwa:)* sparsamer Umgang mit Energie

conserve [kən'sɜːv] 6 erhalten; konservieren; *conserve energy (etwa:)* sparsam mit Energie umgehen

consist [kən'sɪst] 5 *the Eurotunnel consists of two rail tunnels* der Eurotunnel besteht aus zwei Eisenbahntunneln

constant ['kɒnstənt] 7/20 *under constant attack by chemicals* (es wird) dauernd von Chemikalien angegriffen; *the magic constant* die magische Konstante

construct [kən'strʌkt] 5 bauen; erstellen

construction [kən'strʌkʃn] 5/9 Bau; Errichtung; *under construction* im Bau

consume [kən'sjuːm] 12 verbrauchen

consumer [kən'sjuːmə] 7 Verbraucher

consumption [kən'sʌmpʃn] 8 Verbrauch; *petrol consumption* Benzinverbrauch

contact ['kɒntækt] 1/15/16/20 *she'll contact you* sie wird mit Ihnen Verbindung aufnehmen; *business contact* Geschäftsverbindung

contain [kən'teɪn] 9/17/20 enthalten; umfassen; *it contains other patterns* es enthält (auch noch) andere Muster

content ['kɒntent] T2 *the oxygen content* der Sauerstoffgehalt

contents ['kɒntents] T2 Inhalt

continue [kən'tɪnjuː] 14/20 fortsetzen; weitergehen; *they continue to make changes* sie nehmen weiterhin Änderungen vor

contract ['kɒntrækt] 3 Vertrag

contradict [kɒntrə'dɪkt] 17 widersprechen

control [kən'trəʊl] 5/10/12/14/16 Steuerung; Lenkung; Regelung; steuern; lenken; regeln; *control room* Kontrollraum; *automatic control* automatische Steuerung; *we must control pests* wir müssen das Ungeziefer unter Kontrolle halten; *the sensor controls the thickness* der Sensor überwacht die Dicke

convenient [kən'viːnjənt] 7 passend; angenehm

conventions [kən'venʃnz] 3 *thread conventions (etwa:)* Gewindedarstellungen

conversion [kən'vɜːʃn] 16 Umwandlung; Konversion

convert [kən'vɜːt] 8/16 umwandeln

conveyor belt [kən'veɪə belt] 5 Förderband

convince [kən'vɪns] 6 überzeugen

cooker grill oven ['kʊkə 'grɪl ʌvn] 2 Koch- und Grillherd

cooler ['kuːlə] 10 Kühler; Kühleinrichtung

cooling water ['kuːlɪŋ] 10 Kühlwasser

cooperation [kəʊʊpə'reɪʃn] 6/8 Mitarbeit; Zusammenarbeit

copper ['kʊpə] 7/13 Kupfer

core [kɔː] 15 Kern

corrosion [kə'rəʊʒn] 9/T2 Korrosion

count [kaʊnt] 5 zählen; *we're counting on it* wir zählen darauf

counter ['kaʊntə] 13 *at the BA counter* am Schalter der BA

countryside ['kʌntrɪsaɪd] 6 Landschaft; Land

course [kɔːs] T2 *in the course of these developments* im Laufe dieser Entwicklungen

cover ['kʌvə] 2/6/9/12 *under separate cover* mit getrennter Post; *protective covers* Schutzhüllen; *covered with fields of grain* bedeckt mit Kornfeldern; *the top covering* die äußere Schutzschicht; *the outer covering of a tree* die äußere Hülle eines Baumes

crane [kreɪn] 9 Kran

create [kriː'eɪt] 9/T1/12 schaffen; verursachen; *they create an air space* sie schaffen einen Luftraum; *they can create dangers* sie können Gefahren verursachen; *create pulp* Zellstoff erzeugen

credit card ['kredɪt kaːd] 1 Kreditkarte

crooked ['krʊkɪd] 14 krumm

cross [krʊs] 3/5/15 Kreuz; überqueren; *cross the channel* den Kanal überqueren; *cross-shaped* in der Form eines Kreuzes; *cross-hatched* kreuzgerippt; *cross-section* Querschnitt; Schnitt; *cross-sectioning* Querschnittzeichnen

crowded ['kraʊdɪd] 19 voll; überfüllt

crude oil [kruːd] 6 Rohöl

crystalline ['krɪstəlaɪn] 8 Kristall-

current ['kʌrənt] 12/16 Strom; Elektrizität

cursor ['kɜːrsə] A19 Cursor (= *Schreibmarke*)

curve [kɜːv] A4/6 Krümmung; Bogen; *curved* krumm; gebogen

customer ['kʌstəmə] 1 Kunde, Kundin

cut [kʌt] 7/10/11/12/14 *cut up into smaller reels* in kleinere Rollen zerschnitten; *cut down trees* Bäume fällen; *cut off the current* den Strom abschalten; *emissions should be cut in half* (die) Emissionen sollten auf die Hälfte verringert werden; *a 20-per-cent cut* eine zwanzigprozentige Reduzierung; *cut logs* Baumstämme (zer)sägen

cutlery ['kʌtlərɪ] 17 Besteck

cutting head ['kʌtɪŋ] 5 Schneidekopf

cycle ['saɪkl] 12 Zyklus; Schwingung; Turnus; *cycles per second* Schwingungen pro Sekunde

cylinder ['sɪlɪndə] 9 Zylinder

D

damage ['dæmɪdʒ] 14 Schaden; schaden, schädigen; *do damage to the environment* der Umwelt schaden

darkness ['daːknɪs] 4 Dunkelheit

data library ['deɪtə 'laɪbrərɪ] 20 Datenbank, Datenspeicher

data transfer ['deɪtə 'trænsfɜː] 14/16 Datenübertragung

deal [diːl] 5/11 *a great deal of money* eine Menge Geld

debarking [dɪ'baːkɪŋ] 11 Entrinden

decision [dɪ'sɪʒn] 14 Entscheidung

deck [dek] 9 *upper deck* oberes Deck; *number of decks* Zahl der Stockwerke

defective [dɪ'fektɪv] 2/6 defekt

define [dɪ'faɪn] 12 *define something* etwas definieren (festlegen)

degree [dɪ'griː] 3 Grad; *degree of difficulty* Schwierigkeitsgrad

delay [dɪ'leɪ] 10/15 Verzögerung

delivery [dɪ'lɪvərɪ] 2/3 Lieferung

depart [dɪ'paːt] 5 abfahren; abreisen

depend [dɪ'pend] 8 *it depends on the situation* es hängt von der Situation ab; *that depends* das kommt drauf an

depth [depθ] 3 Tiefe

description [dɪ'skrɪpʃn] 1/2 Beschreibung

describe [dɪ'skraɪb] 2 beschreiben

design [dɪˈzaɪn] 2/3/5/12/13 Konstruktion; Entwurf; konstruieren; entwerfen; *the designing process* der Konstruktionsprozeß; *a good design* ein gutes Design

designer [dɪˈzaɪnə] 3 Konstrukteur(in); Designer(in)

despatch [dɪˈspætʃ] *(auch:)* dispatch 16 abschicken; versenden

destroy [dɪˈstrɔɪ] 17 zerstören

destruction [dɪˈstrʌkʃn] 7 Zerstörung

detail [ˈdiːteɪl] 2/3/A19 *some technical details* ein paar technische Einzelheiten; *hidden details* versteckte Einzelheiten; *detailed* detailliert

develop [dɪˈveləp] 4/14/18 entwickeln

developing country [dɪˈveləpɪŋ] T1 Entwicklungsland

development [dɪˈveləpmənt] 4 Entwicklung

device [dɪˈvaɪs] A1 Vorrichtung; Gerät

diagonal [daɪˈægənl] 9 diagonal

diagram [ˈdaɪəgræm] 13 Diagramm; schematische Darstellung

dial [ˈdaɪəl] 17 *please dial 608* bitte wählen Sie 608

dialogue [ˈdaɪəlɒg] 2 Dialog; Gespräch

diameter [daɪˈæmɪtə] 9 Durchmesser

diesel [ˈdiːzl] T2 Diesel(motor)

dig [dɪg] (dug [dʌg] – have dug) graben

diggings [ˈdɪgɪŋz] T1 Lagerstätten *(von Erzen, Edelsteinen etc.)*

digital [ˈdɪdʒɪtl] 4/7 digital

dimension [dɪˈmenʃn] 2/3 Dimension; Abmessung; *dimensioning* Bemaßung; Dimensionierung; *dimensioned according to British standards* Maße entsprechend der britischen Norm

dinette seat [daɪˈnet siːt] 2 *(etwa:)* Sitzplatz mit Eßecke

dip [dɪp] 11/12 (ein)tauchen

direct [dɪˈrekt] 4 *directly from the satellite* direkt vom Satelliten

direction [dɪˈrekʃn] 3 Richtung

dirt [dɜːt] 11 Schmutz

disadvantage [dɪsədˈvɑːntɪdʒ] 2 Nachteil

disaster [dɪˈzɑːstə] 5 Katastrophe

discharge [dɪsˈtʃɑːdʒ] A12 *discharge water* Wasser ablassen

disease [dɪˈziːz] 14 Krankheit

dish [dɪʃ] 4 *(hier:)* Antennenschüssel *(= Parabolantenne)*

disk *(auch:)* disc [dɪsk] 14/A19 *floppy disk* Diskette

diskette [dɪˈsket] A19 Diskette

disperse [dɪˈspɜːs] 11 *the fibres well dispersed* die Fasern gut verteilt

display [dɪˈspleɪ] A19 Anzeige; *(auch:)* Bildschirm; *the goods on display* die gezeigten Waren

disposable [dɪˈspəʊzəbl] 14 Wegwerf-; *disposable paper clothing* Einwegkleidung

distance [ˈdɪstəns] 6 Entfernung; *a long-distance call* ein Ferngespräch

distill [dɪˈstɪl] 10 destillieren

distillation [dɪstɪˈleɪʃn] 10 Destillation

distribute [dɪˈstrɪbjuːt] 12 verteilen

distribution [dɪstrɪˈbjuːʃn] 4 Verteilung; Vertrieb

disturb [dɪˈstɜːb] 17 stören

disturbance [dɪˈstɜːbəns] 14 Störung

divide [dɪˈvaɪd] 20 teilen; aufteilen

do [duː/dʊ] 4/19/20 *do less damage* weniger Schaden verursachen; *do research* forschen; *they did their work on slates* sie machten ihre Hausaufgaben auf Schiefertafeln; *do a better job* bessere Arbeit leisten; *a cafeteria will do* eine Cafeteria wird ausreichen; *will they really do the job?* werden sie wirklich für die Arbeit ausreichen?

document [ˈdɒkjʊmənt] A11 Dokument; Schriftstück

domed roof [dəʊmd] 9 Kuppeldach

double [ˈdʌbl] 20 verdoppeln; doppelt

double glazed [ˈdʌbl ˈgleɪzd] 15 mit Doppelverglasung

downtime [ˈdaʊntaɪm] 12 Ausfallzeit; Stillstandszeit

downtown [ˈdaʊntaʊn] 9 *(US:)* Innenstadt

drain [dreɪn] 12 *drain away water* Wasser abfließen lassen

draw [drɔ:] (drew [dru:] – have drawn [drɔ:n]) *draw a picture* ein Bild zeichnen; *drawing* Zeichnung; *the source from which it was drawn* die Quelle, aus der es stammte

drill [drɪl] 1/2/6 *drill a hole* ein Loch bohren

drill bits [bɪts] 6 Bohrer (= Bohreinsätze)

drill press [pres] 1 Tischbohrmaschine

drilling machine [ˈdrɪlɪŋ] 2 Bohrmaschine

drive [draɪv] 5/8/16 Antrieb; antreiben; *hydrogen drive* Wasserstoffantrieb

drop [drɒp] 12 *drop it in the container* wirf es in den Container

drum [drʌm] 19 Trommel

dump [dʌmp] T1 Müllkippe

duration [djʊəˈreɪʃn] A7 Dauer

dust [dʌst] 10/A11 Staub; Schmutz; *dust bag* Staubbeutel *(eines Staubsaugers)*

dynamo [ˈdaɪnəməʊ] A16 Dynamo, Lichtmaschine

E

earth [ɜ:θ] 4 Erde; erden; *earth wire* Erdung

economical [i:kəˈnɒmɪkl] A18 wirtschaftlich; sparsam

economy [ɪˈkɒnəmɪ] 10 Wirtschaftlichkeit; Wirtschaft; *operational economy* wirtschaftlicher Betrieb

ecosystem [ˈi:kəʊsɪstəm] 11 Ökosystem

edge [ˈedʒ] 11 Kante; Rand

effect [ɪˈfekt] 7/9/14/20 *there was no effect* es zeigte sich keine Wirkung; *data transfer is effected by means of floppy disks* der Datentransfer findet mit Hilfe von Disketten statt; *cause and effect* Ursache und Wirkung; *the greenhouse effect* der Treibhauseffekt; *the effect on the environment* die Wirkung auf die Umwelt

effective [ɪˈfektɪv] T2 wirksam; effektiv

efficiency [ɪˈfɪʃənsɪ] 10 Leistungsfähigkeit; *thermal efficiency* Wärmewirkungsgrad

efficient [ɪˈfɪʃənt] 8/18 leistungsfähig; tüchtig

effort [ˈefət] 15 Anstrengung; *make an effort* sich anstrengen

elastic band [ɪˈlæstɪk] A13 Gummiband

electric [ɪˈlektrɪk] 1/3/14/15/16 *electric shaver* Elektrorasierer; *electric field* elektrisches Feld; *electrical engineer* Elektroingenieur; *electrical fault* Fehler in der Leitung

electrician [ɪlekˈtrɪʃn] 1 Elektriker

electricity [ɪlekˈtrɪsətɪ] T1 Elektrizität

electro-magnet [ɪlektrəʊˈmægnɪt] 16 Elektromagnet

electro-magnetic [ɪlektrəʊmægˈnetɪk] A16 elektromagnetisch

electron [ɪˈlektrɒn] 15 Elektron

electronic [ɪlekˈtrɒnɪk] 16 elektronisch; *electronically controlled* elektronisch gesteuert

electronics [ɪlekˈtrɒnɪks] 11 Elektronik

electroplating [ɪˈlektrəʊpleɪtɪŋ] 17 Elektroplattieren, Galvanisieren

elevator [ˈelɪveɪtə] 15 *(US:)* Aufzug *(GB:* lift)

eliminate [ɪˈlɪmɪneɪt] 10 beseitigen; ausschalten

elimination [ɪlɪmɪˈneɪʃn] 10 Beseitigung; Ausschaltung

emergency [ɪˈmɜːdʒənsɪ] 5 Not-; Notfall; *emergency switch* Notschalter

emission [ɪˈmɪʃn] 7/16 Emission

enable [ɪˈneɪbl] 7 *it will enable them to buy the car* es wird es ihnen ermöglichen, den Wagen zu kaufen

enclose [ɪnˈkləʊz] 16 beifügen; einschließen

enclosure [ɪnˈkləʊʒə] 16 *(hier:)* Anlage

energy [ˈenədʒɪ] 6/12/14 Energie; *energy conservation* Energieerhaltung; Energieeinsparung; *solar energy* Sonnenenergie

engage [ɪnˈɡeɪdʒ] 20 *he's engaged just now (Telefon:)* seine Leitung ist im Moment besetzt

engine [ˈendʒɪn] 18 (Verbrennungs-)Motor

engineer [endʒɪˈnɪə] 1 Ingenieur(in)

enormous [ɪˈnɔːməs] 12 enorm; riesengroß

enter [ˈentə] 10 eintreten; hereinkommen; *air and steam enter* Luft und Dampf strömen herein

entire [ɪnˈtaɪə] 9 *the entire stadium* das ganze Stadion

entry-point [ˈentrɪ] 5 Eintrittsstelle

envelope [ˈenvələʊp] 16 (Brief-)Umschlag

environment [ɪn'vaɪərənmənt] 4 Umwelt

environmental [ɪnvaɪrən'mentl] 7/12 *environmental threat* Bedrohung der Umwelt; *environmental problems* Umweltprobleme; *environmental protection* Umweltschutz

equip [ɪ'kwɪp] T1/13/T2 *they are now equipped with catalytic converters* sie sind jetzt mit Katalysatoren ausgerüstet

equipment [ɪ'kwɪpmənt] 3/16/17 Einrichtung(en); Ausrüstung; Geräte

err [ɜː] 19 *to err is human* irren ist menschlich

escalator ['eskəleɪtə] 13 Rolltreppe

essential [ɪ'senʃl] 10/12 wesentlich; entscheidend; *it's essentially the same* es ist im Grunde genommen das gleiche

establish [ɪ'stæblɪʃ] 17 gründen; einführen; *the company was established in 1873* die Firma wurde im Jahre 1873 gegründet; *they have established a new programme* sie haben ein neues Programm eingeführt

evaluate [ɪ'væljʊeɪt] 8 einschätzen; schätzen

even ['iːvn] 12/13 *an even thickness* eine gleichmäßige Dicke; *it evenly distributes the pulp* es verteilt den Zellstoff gleichmäßig; *make the floor even* den Boden eben machen (= glatt)

eventually [ɪ'ventʃʊəlɪ] 12 schließlich

excavation [ekskə'veɪʃn] T1 Grabung; Ausgrabung

execute ['eksɪkjuːt] A1 durchführen; ausführen; *execute a program* ein Programm durchlaufen lassen

exhaust [ɪg'zɔːst] 16/17 Auspuff; Auspuffgase

exhaust pipe [ɪg'zɔːst] T2 Auspuffrohr

exhibition [eksɪ'bɪʃn] 11 Ausstellung

exist [ɪg'zɪst] 4 bestehen; existieren; *does life exist on other planets?* gibt es Leben auf anderen Planeten?

exit ['eksɪt] 9/11/17 Ausgang; *fire exit* Notausgang *(im Brandfall)*

expand [ɪk'spænd] A4/16 (sich) ausdehnen; erweitern

expansion [ɪk'spænʃn] 12 Ausdehnung; Erweiterung,

expectation [ekspek'teɪʃn] 19 Erwartung

expel [ɪk'spel] 10 ausstoßen; auswerfen

experience [ɪk'spɪərɪəns] 11 Erfahrung; *an experienced programmer* ein erfahrener Programmierer

experiment [ɪk'sperɪmənt] 3/A14 Experiment; experimentieren

explanation [eksplə'neɪʃn] 1 Erklärung, Erläuterung

explosion [ɪk'spləʊʒn] 2 Explosion

explosives [ɪk'spləʊsɪvz] T1 Sprengstoff(e)

expose [ɪk'spəʊz] 2 *do not expose an open flame* benutzen Sie keine offene Flamme

express [ɪk'spres] 3/6 ausdrücken

expression [ɪk'spreʃn] 2 Ausdruck

extension [ɪk'stenʃn] 2/T2 *extension 349* Durchwahl 349; *optional extension* wahlweise Verlängerung

extensive [ɪk'stensɪv] T1 *they are used extensively* sie werden ausgiebig benutzt

exterior wall [ek'stɪərɪə] 15 Außenwand

extinguish [ɪk'stɪŋgwɪʃ] 2 löschen; ausmachen

F

fabric ['fæbrɪk] 9 Stoff

facility [fə'sɪlətɪ] A17 Einrichtung; *washing facility* Wascheinrichtung; *shopping facilities* Einkaufsmöglichkeiten

factor ['fæktə] 8 Faktor; Punkt; *another important factor* noch ein wichtiger Punkt

failure ['feɪljə] 5/14 Fehlschlag; Ausfall; *power failure* Stromausfall

faithfully ['feɪθfʊlɪ] 16 *Yours faithfully (etwa:)* Hochachtungsvoll

fast food ['fɑːst fuːd] 7 Fast food *(= Schnellgerichte wie z. B. Hot Dogs oder Hamburger)*

fasten ['fɑːsn] A9 festmachen; *fasten seat belts* (sich) anschnallen

fault [fɔːlt] 2/5/14 Fehler; *a fault in the program* ein Fehler im Programm; *electrical fault* elektrischer Fehler; *whose fault was it?* wer war schuld daran? *it's my fault* es ist mein Fehler

favour ['feɪvə] 7/20 *they are in favour of cleaning up the environment* sie sind dafür, die Umwelt zu säubern; *I'm not very much* *in favour of his proposals* ich bin von seinen Vorschlägen nicht besonders angetan

fax/fax machine [fæks] 3/A16/19 Faxgerät

feature ['fi:tʃə] 15 Eigenschaft; Merkmal; *the main features* die Hauptmerkmale; *it features a new chip* das hervorstechende Merkmal ist ein neuer Chip

fell [fel] 11 *fell trees* Bäume fällen

felt [felt] 12 Filz

fertilize ['fɜ:tɪlaɪz] 14 düngen

fertilizer ['fɜ:tɪlaɪzə] 4 Dünger

fibre (*US:* fiber) ['faɪbə] A4/8/A9 Faser; *fibre optics* Faseroptik; *fibre-reinforced carbon* faserverstärkter Kohlenstoff

fibrillate ['faɪbrɪleɪt] 11 schütteln

figure ['fɪgə] 11/19 Zahl; Figur

filament ['fɪləmənt] A16/16 Faden; Filament; Glühfaden

file [faɪl] 1 Feile

fill [fɪl] 1/2/17 *fill the tank* tanken; *fill valve* Füllstutzen; *fill in a form* ein Formular ausfüllen

filling station ['fɪlɪŋ] T1 Tankstelle

filter ['fɪltə] 12/18 Filter; filtern

finish ['fɪnɪʃ] T2 Ende; beenden; fertigstellen

firm ['fɜ:m] 11 fest

fit [fɪt] 1/5/18 passen

fittings ['fɪtɪŋz] T2 Armaturen

flame [fleɪm] 2 Flamme

fix [fɪks] 5/9/15/17 reparieren; festmachen; *can you fix it?* können Sie es reparieren? *it needs fixing* es muß repariert werden; *a fixed link* eine feste Verbindung; *fix something to the wall* etwas an der Wand festmachen

flammable ['flæməbl] 2 feuergefährlich; leicht entzündlich

flat [flæt] 6/10/11 *the countryside was flat* das Land war flach; *a flat tire (US:)* eine Reifenpanne (*GB:* puncture); *flat belt* Flachriemen; *lift the mesh up flat* das Siebgeflecht flach hochheben

fleet [fli:t] 8 Wagenpark; Flotte

flexibility [fleksə'bɪlətɪ] 15 Elastizität; Flexibilität

flexible ['fleksəbl] 12/16 biegsam; elastisch; flexibel

flood [flʌd] 5 Flut; überfluten; *flooded with light* lichtdurchflutet

floor plan ['flɔ: plæn] 2 Grundriß (*eines Stockwerks*)

floppy disk ['flɒpɪ dɪsk] 14 Diskette

flow [fləʊ] 2/10/15/16/17 *it flows through channels* es fließt durch Kanäle; *when the current flows* wenn der Strom fließt; *they flow into the water* sie fließen ins Wasser; *gas flow* Gasstrom

flowsheet ['fləʊʃi:t] 10 Flußdiagramm

fluid ['flu:ɪd] 10 Flüssigkeit; flüssig

foam [fəʊm] 7 Schaum

football ['fʊtbɔ:l] A9 Fußball

forbid [fɔ'bɪd] 4 verbieten

force [fɔ:s] 14 Stärke; Kraft; zwingen; *force people to recycle forest products* die Leute dazu zwingen, Holzprodukte wiederzuverwerten; *it forces the valve to open* es zwingt das Ventil, sich zu öffnen

foreman ['fɔ:mən] 20 (*etwa:*) Werkmeister; (*auch:*) Vorarbeiter

forest ['fɒrɪst] 11/14 Wald

forestry retraining centre ['fɒrɪstrɪ] 14 forstwirtschaftliches Umschulungszentrum

fork-lift truck ['fɔ:k lɪft] 9 Gabelstapler

form [fɔ:m] 4/8/11/12/17 *life forms* Lebensformen; *the original form* die ursprüngliche Form; *they form the roof* sie bilden das Dach; *in the form of gas* gasförmig; *form a sheet of paper* ein Blatt Papier bilden; *fill in a form* ein Formular ausfüllen

former ['fɔ:mə] 15 früher; ehemalig; *in former times* früher

formula ['fɔ:mjulə] 20 Formel

formulation [fɔ:mju'leɪʃn] 16 *mixture formulation* Mischungsformulierung

fossil fuel ['fɒsl fjʊəl] 5 fossiler Brennstoff

foul [faʊl] 19 *to really foul things up* um die Dinge wirklich ganz durcheinander zu bringen

fragile ['frædʒaɪl] 4 zerbrechlich

frame [freɪm] 12 Rahmen; rahmen

fray [freɪ] 11 *fray the edges of the fibres* die Kanten der Fasern zerfransen

freight [freɪt] 5 Fracht; Güter-

frequent ['friːkwənt] 12 oft; häufig

friction ['frɪkʃn] 12 Reibung; Friktion; *friction heat* Reibungswärme

fridge → refrigerator

fuel ['fjʋəl] 2/5/10/13/16 *fuel tank* Treibstofftank; *fossil fuel* fossiler Brennstoff; *industrial fuel gas* industrielles Brenngas; *fuel oil products* Heizölprodukte; *aircraft fuel* Flugbenzin; *fuel consumption* Treibstoffverbrauch

function ['fʌŋkʃn] 13 Funktion; funktionieren

functional space ['fʌŋkʃənl] 15 Zweckraum (= *Raum für bestimmte Aufgaben*)

fusing area ['fjuːzɪŋ] 19 *(hier:)* Fixierer

G

galaxy ['gæləksɪ] 4 Galaxie

galvanize ['gælvənaɪz] 9 verzinken; galvanisieren

gap [gæp] T1 Lücke

garbage ['gɑːbɪdʒ] 7/12 *(hauptsächlich US)* Abfall; Müll; *garbage can* Abfalleimer; *garbage man* Müllmann; *garbage collector* Müllmann

gas [gæs] 2/7/10 Gas

gas [gæs] (= gasoline ['gæsəuliːn]) 7 *(US:)* Benzin (*GB:* petrol)

gasification [gæsɪfɪ'keɪʃn] 10 Vergasung

gasifier ['gæsɪfaɪə] 10 (industrielle) Vergasungsanlage

gasify ['gæsɪfaɪ] 10 vergasen

gasoline → gas

gate [geɪt] 6 Gatter; Sperre; Tor

gauge (*US auch:* gage) [geɪdʒ] 2 Meßgerät; Anzeiger; *petrol gauge* Benzinuhr; *tank gauge* Tankanzeiger; *oil gauge* Ölstandsanzeiger

gears [gɪəz] 1/A18 Zahnräder; Getriebe

gear shift ['gɪə ʃɪft] A18 *(Auto:)* Schalthebel

gear wheel [gɪə] 1 Zahnrad

generate ['dʒenəreɪt] 10/16 erzeugen

generator ['dʒenəreɪtə] 2 Generator; Lichtmaschine

get [get] 3/7/8/11/14/16 *get it right* es richtig hinkriegen; *get rid of garbage* Müll loswerden; *they got that engine repaired very quickly* sie schafften es, den Motor sehr schnell zu reparieren; *get through* durchkommen; *get hot* warm/heiß werden; *get up early* früh aufstehen; *there's got to be an easier way* es muß einen leichteren Weg geben

go [gəʊ] 5/10/11/12/16 *go into operation* in Betrieb gehen; *nothing goes to waste* nichts geht verloren; *coal goes down* die Kohle fällt herunter; *and then it goes into a vat* und dann geht sie in eine Bütte

goal [gəʊl] 12 Ziel; Tor

gold [gəʊld] 17 Gold

gradual ['grædʒʋəl] 10 allmählich; *gradually increasing* allmählich ansteigend

grain [greɪn] 6 Getreide

graph [græf] T2 grafische Darstellung

graphics ['græfɪks] 20 grafische Darstellungen; Grafiken

grease [griːs] 20 Schmierfett; fetten

greenfield site ['griːnfiːld saɪt] A12 Standort „auf der grünen Wiese"

greenhouse ['griːnhaʋs] 5/7 Treibhaus; Gewächshaus; *greenhouse effect* Treibhauseffekt

greeting ['griːtɪŋ] 2 Gruß; Begrüßung

grid [grɪd] 9 Rost; Gitter(netz)

grow [grəʊ] (grew [gruː] – have grown [grəʊn]) 8/12/14 wachsen; anpflanzen; züchten; *grow trees* Bäume anpflanzen; *the use of recycled waste paper has grown* die Verwendung von wiederverwertetem Abfallpapier ist gestiegen; *growing competition* wachsende Konkurrenz

growth [grəʊθ] 14 Wachstum

grub screw [grʌb] 3 Gewindestift

H

habit ['hæbɪt] 6 Gewohnheit; *a bad habit* eine schlechte Angewohnheit

halogen lamp [ˈhælədʒen læmp] T1 Halogenlampe

hammer [ˈhæmə] 3 Hammer; hämmern

hand [hænd] 9/11 *on the one hand/on the other hand* einerseits/andererseits; *hand made paper* handgeschöpftes Papier

handkerchief [ˈhæŋkətʃif] A11 Taschentuch

handle [ˈhændl] 10/16 *easy to handle* leicht zu handhaben; *pull handle* Zuggriff; *pull the handle* ziehen Sie den Griff

handsaw [ˈhændsɔ:] 14 Handsäge

hang on a minute [hæŋ] 20 bleiben Sie am Apparat

hard hat [ˈhɑ:d hæt] 5 Schutzhelm

harden [ˈhɑ:dn] A17 härten

hardware [ˈhɑ:dweə] 1 Hardware (= *technische Einrichtungen elektronischer Rechenanlagen*)

harm [hɑ:m] *harm the environment* die Umwelt schädigen; *come to harm* zu Schaden kommen

harmful [ˈhɑ:mfʊl] 17 schädlich

harvest [ˈhɑ:vɪst] 14 Ernte; ernten

hatching lines [ˈhætʃɪŋ] 3 schraffierte Linien

head [hed] 5/17 Kopf; Haupt-; *cutting head* Schneidekopf

headquarters [ˈhedkwɔ:təz] *(etwa:)* Zentrale

health [helθ] 8 Gesundheit

healthy [ˈhelθɪ] 7 gesund

heat [hi:t] 6/11/12 *turn down the heat (etwa:)* die Heizung niedriger stellen; *fluids are heated* die Flüssigkeiten werden erhitzt; *heat energy* Wärmeenergie; *heat treatment* Wärmebehandlung

height [haɪt] 2 Höhe

helmet [ˈhelmɪt] 5 Helm

hesitate [ˈhezɪteɪt] 16 zögern

hi-fi equipment [ˈhaɪfaɪ] 3 Hi-Fi-Geräte (hi-fi = *high fidelity* [fɪˈdelətɪ] hohe Tontreue)

high level storage locker 2 obenliegender Stauraum

high-pressure steam [ˈhaɪpreʃə] 16 Hochdruckdampf

high-speed steel bit [ˈhaɪspi:d] 1 Bohreinsätze aus Schnellarbeitsstahl

high protein woodburgers [ˈhaɪ ˈprəʊti:n] 14 *(etwa:)* Hamburger mit hohem Proteingehalt aus Holzstoff

high-vacuum technology [ˈhaɪ ˈvækjʊəm] A17 Hochvakuumtechnologie

hiker [ˈhaɪkə] 13 Wanderer

hillside [hɪlˈsaɪd] 14 Hang

hire [ˈhaɪə] 14 mieten; *(Leute:)* anstellen, beschäftigen, einstellen

historic [hɪˈstɒrɪk] 7 historisch

hi-tech [ˈhaɪˈtek] 18 High-Tech (= *Hochtechnologie*)

hold [həʊld] (held [held] – have held) halten; festhalten; *hold a meeting* eine Versammlung abhalten; *they cannot be held responsible* man kann sie nicht verantwortlich machen; *hold on a moment (Telefon:)* warten Sie einen Moment; *hold the line (Telefon:)* bleiben Sie am Apparat

hole [həʊl] 1 Loch

hollow [ˈhɒləʊ] 11 hohl

hookup [ˈhʊkʌp] 2/A2 *full hookups (US:)* volle Anschlüsse (= *das Reisemobil wird am Standort an die Abwasser-, Frischwasser- und Stromversorgung angeschlossen*)

horsehead pumps [ˈhɔ:shed] 6 *wörtlich:* „Pferdekopfpumpen" (= *weil sie wie Pferdeköpfe aussehen*) Tiefpumpen; Plungerpumpen

horsemen [ˈhɔ:smen] 13 Reiter

hose [həʊz] 12 Schlauch

house [haʊz] 15 unterbringen; beherbergen; *it houses the elevator system* in ihm ist das Fahrstuhlsystem untergebracht; *... to house all the systems ...* um alle Systeme unterzubringen

household [ˈhaʊshəʊld] 8 Haushalt

housing problem [ˈhaʊzɪŋ] 5 Wohnungsproblem

hovercraft [ˈhɒvəkrɑ:ft] 5/T2 Hovercraft; Luftkissenboot

huge [hju:dʒ] 14 riesig

human [ˈhju:mən] 4/8 *a human operator* ein Mensch als Bedienungskraft; *human beings* Menschen

humid ['hjuːmɪd] 5 feucht

hurricane ['hʌrɪkən] 5 Hurrikan, Orkan

hydrocarbons [haɪdrəʊ'kaːbənz] 16 Kohlen-wasserstoffe

hydro-electric ['haɪdrəʊ-ɪ'lektrɪk] 7/12/14 hy-droelektrisch; *hydro-electric power station* Wasserkraftwerk

hydrogen ['haɪdrədʒən] 8 Wasserstoff

hydrogen peroxide ['haɪdrədʒən pə'rɒksaɪd] 12/A12 Wasserstoffperoxid

hydraulic [haɪ'drɔːlɪk] A18 hydraulisch

I

icon ['aɪkɒn] A19 *(Computer:)* Ikon (= *klei-nes Bild oder Symbol)*

icy roads ['aɪsɪ] 3 vereiste Straßen

identify [aɪ'dentɪfaɪ] 3/12 identifizieren; be-stimmen; erkennen; *can the computer identify this?* kann der Computer das er-kennen?

ignition [ɪg'nɪʃn] T2 Zündung

illustrate ['ɪləstreɪt] 2 illustrieren; bildlich dar-stellen; zeigen

impression [ɪm'preʃn] 10 Eindruck

impurity [ɪm'pjʊərətɪ] 12 Verunreinigung

incineration [ɪnsɪnə'reɪʃn] 12 Verbrennung; *incineration plant (incinerator)* Verbren-nungsofen *(z. B. für Abfälle)*

inconvenience [ɪnkən'viːnjəns] A7/13 Unan-nehmlichkeit

increase ['ɪnkriːs] T2 Steigerung; Erhöhung

increase [ɪn'kriːs] 5/10/12 steigern; erhöhen; *increasing temperatures* steigende Tempe-raturen

independent [ɪndɪ'pendənt] 15 unabhängig

indicate ['ɪndɪkeɪt] 3 anzeigen; *indicate the outlines of a project* ein Projekt umreißen

industrial [ɪn'dʌstrɪəl] 1/10/12 industriell; In-dustrie-

inflatable [ɪn'fleɪtəbl] 9 aufblasbar

infrastructure ['ɪnfrəstrʌktʃə] A12 Infrastruk-tur

ingredients [ɪn'griːdjənts] 12 Bestandteile; Zu-taten

initial [ɪ'nɪʃl] 15 Anfangs-

input ['ɪnpʊt] 1 Eingabe, Input

insect ['ɪnsekt] A14 Insekt

install [ɪn'stɔːl] 1/10/11/14 einbauen; instal-lieren

installation [ɪnstə'leɪʃn] 4/9 Einbau; Installa-tion

instant starch ['ɪnstənt 'staːtʃ] 11 Instant-stärke

institution [ɪnstɪ'tjuːʃn] 8 Einrichtung; Institu-tion

instructions [ɪn'strʌkʃnz] 1/9 Anweisungen; *operating instructions* Bedienungsanlei-tung, Betriebsanweisung

insulate ['ɪnsjʊleɪt] 12 isolieren

insulation [ɪnsjʊ'leɪʃn] 9 Isolierung; *thermal insulation* Wärmeisolierung

integrate ['ɪntɪgreɪt] A18 integrieren

inter-connected pillows [ɪntəkə'nektɪd] 9 mit-einander verbundene Kissen

interface ['ɪntəfeɪs] 5/20/T2 Schnittstelle; Ver-bindung; verbinden

interior [ɪn'tɪərɪə] 2/9 *interior height* Innen-höhe; *interior volume* Innenvolumen

intermediate [ɪntə'miːdjət] 15/A17 *interme-diate levels* Zwischengeschosse; *interme-diate products* Zwischenprodukte

internal combustion engine [ɪn'tɜːnl] 12 Ver-brennungsmotor, Ottomotor

internal thread [θred] 3 Innengewinde

interrupt [ɪntə'rʌpt] 5 unterbrechen

interstate highway ['ɪntəsteɪt] 13 *(US:)* Auto-bahn

interview ['ɪntəvjuː] 5 Interview; Vorstellungs-gespräch; (jemand) interviewen, befragen

introduce [ɪntrə'djuːs] 2/12 einführen; vorstel-len

introduction [ɪntrə'dʌkʃn] 1 Einführung; Vor-stellung

invent [ɪn'vent] 12 erfinden

inventor [ɪn'ventə] 3 Erfinder

invest [ɪn'vest] 12 investieren

investigation [ɪnvestɪ'geɪʃn] 15 Untersuchung; Überprüfung

investment [ɪn'vestmənt] 8 Investition

invitation [ɪnvɪ'teɪʃn] 10 Einladung

involve [ɪn'vɒlv] 5/8 *the dangers involved* die damit verbundenen Gefahren; *experiments which involve powering vehicles by hydrogen drive* Experimente, die darauf hinauslaufen, Fahrzeuge mit Wasserstoffantrieb auszustatten; *she was involved in the project* sie war an dem Projekt beteiligt; *the car was involved in the accident* der Wagen war in den Unfall verwickelt

iron ['aɪən] A9 Eisen

iron oxide ['aɪən 'ɒksaɪd] A19 Eisenoxid

item ['aɪtəm] 11/17 Sache; Punkt; Artikel; Gegenstand; *an interesting news item* eine interessante Nachricht; *all the items on this list* alle Posten auf dieser Liste

J

jet [dʒet] 14/18 Strahl; Düsenflugzeug; *water jet* Wasserstrahl

jewellery industry ['dʒuːəlrɪ] 17 Schmuckindustrie

join [dʒɔɪn] 3/9/10 *join something to the other end* etwas am anderen Ende festmachen; *join the ends* die Enden miteinander verbinden; *would you like to join us for dinner?* möchten Sie gerne mit uns zu Abend essen? *...which joins with the distillation vapours ...* welches sich mit den Destillationsdämpfen verbindet

journal ['dʒɜːnl] 1 Zeitschrift

just [dʒʌst] *a just man* ein gerechter Mann

justify ['dʒʌstɪfaɪ] 14 *this cannot be justified* das ist nicht zu rechtfertigen

K

keep [kiːp] (kept [kept] – have kept) halten; festhalten; *keep it an even thickness* auf gleichmäßige Dicke halten; *it keeps the cable attached* es hält das Kabel fest

kerb weight [kɜːb] A8 Leergewicht (*kerb* = Bordstein)

key [kiː] A1 Taste; Schlüssel

keyboard ['kiːbɔːd] A1 Tastatur

kiosk ['kiːɒsk] 13 Kiosk

knot [nɒt] 14 Knoten; knoten

L

labour-saving machines ['leɪbə] T1 arbeitssparende Maschinen

laden ['leɪdn] A8 beladen

lambda sensor ['læmdə] 16 Lambdasonde (*= Meßfühler in Ottomotoren zur Regelung der Gemischbildung*)

laser ['leɪzə] 5/16 Laser

launch [lɔːntʃ] 4/15 *the launch into space* der Start in den Weltraum; *launch a satellite* einen Satelliten hochschießen; *launch a new product* ein neues Produkt auf den Markt bringen; *launch a ship* ein Schiff vom Stapel lassen

lawn-mower ['lɔːn-məʊə] T1 Rasenmäher

layer ['leɪə] 7/9 Schicht

leaflet ['liːflɪt] 14 Prospekt; Merkblatt

leak [liːk] 2 *there's a leak in the tank* der Tank hat ein Leck; *I can smell a gas leak* hier riecht es nach Gas; *the roof leaks* das Dach ist undicht

lean [liːn] 8 mager; *lean production (etwa:)* kostengünstige Produktion; *lean engine* Magermotor

level ['levl] 2/4/9/13/15 *check the oil level* den Ölstand prüfen; *departure level* Abflughalle; *intermediate levels* Zwischengeschosse; *the motorhome is level* das Reisemobil steht gerade

lever ['liːvə; US 'levə] T1/A19 Hebel

light bulb ['laɪt bʌlb] 4 Glühlampe, Glühbirne

limitation [lɪmɪ'teɪʃn] A8 Begrenzung

line [laɪn] 20 *hold the line* bleiben Sie dran (*= am Telefon*); *the line is busy* die Leitung ist besetzt

link [lɪŋk] 5 *linking Britain and France* Großbritannien und Frankreich verbindend; *a service tunnel is linked to them* ein Servicetunnel ist mit ihnen verbunden; *a fixed link* eine feste Verbindung; *dig the links* die Verbindungstunnel graben

liquid ['lɪkwɪd] 9 Flüssigkeit

litter ['lɪtə] 7 Abfall; *no littering!* keine Abfälle wegwerfen!

loan [ləʊn] 12 Darlehen

local agent [ˈləʊkl] 15 örtlicher Vertreter

locate [ləʊˈkeɪt] 9/12 *where the stadium is located* wo sich das Stadion befindet; *the switch is located at the rear* der Schalter befindet sich hinten

location [ləʊˈkeɪʃn] 10 Standort; Lage; Position

lock [lɒk] 11 *lock the fibres together* die Fasern miteinander verbinden; *door lock* Türschloß; *lock the door* die Tür abschließen

locksmith [ˈlɒksmɪθ] 1 Schlosser

lodging [ˈlɒdʒɪŋ] 13 Unterkunft

log [lɒg] 11/14 Holz schlagen; *this forest has never been logged* in diesem Wald ist nie Holz geschlagen worden

logger [ˈlɒgə] 14 Holzfäller; Holzarbeiter, Waldarbeiter

logging [ˈlɒgɪŋ] 11/14 Holzeinschlag, Holzfällen

logical [ˈlɒdʒɪkl] 6 logisch

look [lʊk] 8 *look after something* sich um etwas kümmern

loose [luːs] T1/12 lose

lorry [ˈlɒrɪ] (*US:* truck) A5 Lastwagen

lose [luːz] (lost [lost] – have lost) 3/13 *he lost his job* er hat seine Arbeit verloren; *I've lost my way* ich habe mich verlaufen

lot [lɒt] 13 *the lot never closes* der Parkplatz ist immer geöffnet

lounge [laʊndʒ] A6 (*hier:*) Hotelhalle

lubricate [ˈluːbrɪkeɪt] 18/20 schmieren

lubrication [luːbrɪˈkeɪʃn] 20 Schmierung

lumber [ˈlʌmbə] A14 Holz

lump [lʌmp] 11 Klumpen; Brocken

luxury [ˈlʌkʃərɪ] 2 Luxus

M

machinery [məˈʃiːnərɪ] 5 Maschinen

machining centre (*US:* center) [məˈʃiːnɪŋ] Bearbeitungszentrum (*= eine hochentwickelte Vielzweckmaschine*)

magazine [mægəˈziːn] A11 (*hier:*) Zeitschrift, Illustrierte

magic [ˈmædʒɪk] 20 *magic squares* magische Quadrate; *the magic constant* die magische Konstante

magnet [ˈmægnɪt] A16 Magnet

magnetic stripe [mægˈnetɪk ˈstraɪp] 6 Magnetstreifen

magnify [ˈmægnɪfaɪ] 8 vergrößern; *magnified by 270:1* zweihundertsiebzigfach vergrößert

mains [meɪnz] T1/A15 Stromnetz; *mains failure* Netzausfall; *mains frequency* Netzfrequenz

maintain [meɪnˈteɪn] 11 *this car is expensive to maintain* dieser Wagen ist teuer im Unterhalt; *maintain a machine* eine Maschine instandhalten; *maintain a conversation* eine Unterhaltung in Fluß halten

maintenance [ˈmeɪntənəns] 2/5/16 Instandhaltung; *maintenance engineer* Wartungsingenieur; *routine maintenance* routinemäßige Wartung

major [ˈmeɪdʒə] 7 *a major conference (etwa:)* eine bedeutende Konferenz

maneuver [məˈnuːvə] T2 manövrieren

manual [ˈmænjʊəl] 1/4 Handbuch; *operating manual* Bedienungsanleitung; Betriebsanleitung

manufacture [mænjʊˈfæktʃə] 9 Herstellung; herstellen

manufacturer [mænjʊˈfaktʃərə] 12 Hersteller

mark [mɑːk] 5/13/A17 *trails marked with these symbols* Wege, die mit diesem Symbol markiert sind; *mark a, b, c or d* markieren Sie a, b, c oder d; *is marked by…* wird charakterisiert durch…

market [ˈmɑːkɪt] 3 *market a product* ein Produkt auf den Markt bringen; *changes in the market-place* Änderungen des Marktes

market research [ˈmɑːkɪt rɪˈsɜːtʃ] A3 Marktforschung

marketing [ˈmɑːkɪtɪŋ] 2/16 Marketing (*= alle Maßnahmen eines Unternehmens, die darauf ausgerichtet sind, den Absatz zu fördern*)

marvellous [ˈmɑːvələs] 8 fantastisch

mass [mæs] 12 Masse

match [mætʃ] A10/T1 *match the explanations to the pictures* ordnen Sie die Erläuterungen den Abbildungen zu; *light a match* ein Streichholz anzünden

mathematician [mæθəmə'tɪʃn] 3 Mathematiker(in)

mathematics [mæθə'mætɪks] T2 Mathematik

matter ['mætə] 4/8/18 *that would be another matter* das wäre eine andere Sache; *your help in this matter* Ihre Hilfe in dieser Angelegenheit; *as a matter of fact* in der Tat; *it doesn't matter* es spielt keine Rolle

maximum ['mæksɪməm] 9/10 Maximum; Maximal-

means → by means of

measure ['meʒə] 4/16 messen

measurement ['meʒəmənt] 7 Messung; Maß

mechanic [mɪ'kænɪk] 1/9 Mechaniker

mechanical [mɪ'kænɪkl] 1/9/11/15 *mechanical engineer* Maschinenbauingenieur; *mechanical breakdown* technische Panne; *mechanical system* technisches System; *mechanical pulp* Holzschliff (= *holzhaltiger Zellstoff*)

medicine ['medsɪn] 4/A5 Medizin

meet [miːt] (met [met] – have met) 3/5 *does it meet the standard?* entspricht es der Norm? *the tunnels meet up under the Channel* die Tunnel treffen unter dem Kanal zusammen

melt [melt] 10 schmelzen

memo ['meməʊ] (= memorandum [meməˈrændəm]) 2 Notiz; Mitteilung

memory metal ['memərɪ] 8 Memorymetall; Memorylegierung (= *Metall mit Formerinnerungsvermögen*)

mesh [meʃ] 11 Geflecht; Masche; Netzgewebe

metal shears ['metl 'ʃɪəz] 1 Metallschere

mid-Channel ['mɪd-'tʃænl] 5 *in mid-Channel* in der Mitte des Kanals

mid-range ['mɪd-reɪndʒ] 19 im mittleren Bereich

mill [mɪl] 11/12 Fabrik; Mühle; *paper mill* Papierfabrik, Papiermühle; *pulp mill* Zellstoffabrik

milling machine ['mɪlɪŋ] 11 Fräsmaschine

mine [maɪn] T1/16 Bergwerk; Mine; *open mine shafts* Schächte der Tagebauminen; *coal mine* Kohlebergwerk; *mining* der Bergbau; *opal mining* Opalabbau; *mining machinery* Bergbaumaschinen

miner ['maɪnə] T1 Bergmann

minimize ['mɪnɪmaɪz] 10 *minimize staff* die Belegschaft auf ein Mindestmaß beschränken

minimum ['mɪnɪməm] 15/T2 *with minimum work* mit möglichst wenig Arbeit; *minimum requirements* Mindestanforderungen

minutes ['mɪnɪts] 19 Protokoll (*einer Sitzung oder Besprechung*)

mirror ['mɪrə] 17 Spiegel

missing ['mɪsɪŋ] 13/20 *the missing word* das fehlende Wort; *some of the numbers are missing* einige der Zahlen fehlen

mix [mɪks] 11/12 Mischung; mischen; *mixing vat* Mischbütte

mixture ['mɪkstʃə] 10 Mischung

model ['mɒdl] 1/14 Modell; Muster

modernization [mɒdənaɪ'zeɪʃn] 12 Modernisierung

modernize ['mɒdənaɪz] A14 modernisieren

modification [mɒdɪfɪ'keɪʃn] T2 Abänderung; Modifizierung

modify ['mɒdɪfaɪ] T2 abändern; modifizieren

module ['mɒdjuːl] 5 Modul; Bauelement

mole [məʊl] 5 (*eigentlich:*) Maulwurf; (*hier:*) Tunnelbohrmaschine

molecule ['mɒlɪkjuːl] A5 Molekül

monitor ['mɒnɪtə] 5/A12/16 *monitor a machine* eine Maschine überwachen; *oxygen-monitoring device* Sauerstoff-Überwachungsanlage; *computer monitor* Computermonitor (= *Bildschirm*)

moon [muːn] 13 Mond

motel [məʊ'tel] 13 Motel

motion ['məʊʃn] 13 Bewegung

motor ['məʊtə] 1 Motor

motor bike ['məʊtə baɪk] 13/16 Motorrad

motorhome ['məʊtəhəʊm] A1/2/T2 Reisemobil

motor vehicle ['məʊtə viːɪkəl] 8 Kraftfahrzeug

motor inn ['məʊtə 'ɪn] 17 Motel

motorisation [məʊtəraɪ'zeɪʃn] T2 Motorisierung

moulding ['məʊldɪŋ] A20 Formen; *moulding material* Formmasse

mount [maʊnt] 12 montieren; festspannen; auf/anbauen; *mounted at the rear* hinten montiert

mouse [maʊs] 4 Maus; Computermaus

movable ['muːvəbl] 15 beweglich

move [muːv] 2/9/12/15 bewegen; versetzen; befördern; umziehen; *move the worktable up and down* den Arbeitstisch auf und ab bewegen; *the paper was moved to another room* das Papier wurde in einen anderen Raum gebracht; *moving electrons* sich bewegende Elektronen

mȯvie ['muːvɪ] 14 *(hauptsächlich US:)* Film; *go to the movies* ins Kino gehen

mow [məʊ] 14 *mow the weeds* das Unkraut mähen

multiply ['mʌltɪplaɪ] A20 multiplizieren; vervielfältigen

mushy ['mʌʃɪ] 11 matschig; breiig

N

native people ['neɪtɪv] 13/14 Ureinwohner; *(hier:)* Indianer

network ['netwɜːk] A19 Netz; Netzwerk; Sender

newsprint ['njuːzprɪnt] A11 Zeitungspapier

nickel ['nɪkl] 7 Nickel

nitrogen oxide ['naɪtrədʒən 'ɒksaɪd] 16/T2 Stickstoffoxid

nominal ['nɒmɪnl] A8 nominell; *nominal value* Nominalwert, Nennwert *(= auf dem Leistungsschild oder im Handbuch genannter Wert)*

non-metallic ['nɒn-mɪ'tælɪk] A10 nichtmetallisch

nonsense ['nɒnsəns] 4 Unsinn

norm [nɔːm] 18 Norm; Standard

note [nəʊt] 3 Anmerkung; Notiz; *take/make notes* Notizen machen

notice ['nəʊtɪs] T1/11/15 *he hardly noticed me* er bemerkte mich kaum; *I immediately noticed that…* ich bemerkte sofort, daß…

nuclear power ['njuːklɪə] 7/15 Atomkraft

numeric [njuː'merɪk] A1 numerisch

nursing floors ['nɜːsɪŋ] 15 *(hier:)* Behandlungs- und Pflegeräume *(des Krankenhauses)*

nut [nʌt] 1 Mutter *(für eine Schraube)*

O

object ['ɒbdʒɪkt] 3 Gegenstand; Objekt

obstruct [əb'strʌkt] 5/9 versperren; blockieren; verstopfen

official [ə'fɪʃl] 13 *(etwa:)* Beamter/Beamtin; "Offizielle(r)" *(z. B. von einem Amt oder einer Institution)*

off-line ['ɒflaɪn] 20 Off-line *(= Begriff aus der Datenverarbeitung für nicht vom Rechner gesteuerte Peripheriegeräte)*

oil [ɔɪl] 6/10 Öl; ölen

on [ɒn] 7/9/10/T1/11/13/16 *on balance* alles in allem; *on schedule* planmäßig; *on top* oben; *on a large scale* in großem Maße; *on request* auf Wunsch; *on the one hand/on the other hand* einerseits/andererseits; *deliver on time* pünktlich liefern; *on average* im Durchschnitt; *wheels with teeth on them* Räder mit Zähnen; *on this problem* zu diesem Problem

opal ['əʊpl] T1 Opal *(= Schmuckstein)*

open mine shaft T1 Tagebauschacht

operate ['ɒpəreɪt] 4/5/16/T2 *operated by the pressure of water* vom Wasserdruck angetrieben; *operate a production plant* eine Produktionsanlage betreiben; *this appliance operates on batteries* dieses Gerät arbeitet mit Batterien

operating manual ['ɒpəreɪtɪŋ] 4 Betriebsanleitung

operating system ['ɒpəreɪtɪŋ] 5 Betriebssystem

operation [ɒpə'reɪʃn] 2/5/10/15/T2 *the operation of the system* der Betrieb des Systems; *go into operation* in Betrieb gehen; *a simple clean-up operation* ein einfacher

Säuberungsvorgang; *the machine has been in operaton since last Monday* die Maschine ist seit letztem Montag in Betrieb

operational economy [ɒpəˈreɪʃənl] 10 wirtschaftlicher Betrieb

operator [ˈɒpəreɪtə] 2/T1/15/20 *(etwa:)* Maschinenbediener; Bedienungskraft

opposite [ˈɒpəzɪt] 3 gegenüberliegend; entgegengesetzt

optic/optical [ˈɒptɪk/ˈɒptɪkl] A4/8 optisch

option [ˈɒpʃn] 19 Wahlmöglichkeit; Wahl; Option

optional [ˈɒpʃənl] 2 wahlweise erhältlich *(gegen Aufpreis, als Zusatzeinrichtung)*

oral [ˈɔːrəl] 11 mündlich

orbit [ˈɔːbɪt] A4 *in orbit* in der Umlaufbahn; *in orbit around the moon* in der Mondumlaufbahn; *send into orbit* in die Umlaufbahn bringen; *the satellite is orbiting the moon* der Satellit umkreist gerade den Mond

orchard [ˈɔːtʃəd] 14 Obstgarten

order [ˈɔːdə] 1/5/9/10/11/12/A20 *in order of importance* in der Reihenfolge der Wichtigkeit; *he gives the orders* er gibt die Befehle (Anweisungen); *in the correct order* in der richtigen Reihenfolge; *the machine is out of order* die Maschine funktioniert nicht; *you ordered a machine last week* Sie haben vorige Woche eine Maschine bestellt; *order form* Bestellformular; *order number* Auftragsnummer

outer layer [ˈaʊtə] 9 äußere Schicht

outline [ˈaʊtlaɪn] 3 Umriß

output [ˈaʊtpʊt] T1/A19 Produktion; Output; Förderung, Fördermenge

overall length [ˈəʊvərɔːl ˈleŋθ] 2 Gesamtlänge; Länge über alles

overfill [əʊvəˈfɪl] 2 zu voll machen

overflow valve [ˈəʊvəfləʊ] 2 Überlaufventil

overloaded [əʊvəˈləʊdɪd] A13 überlastet

overnight [əʊvəˈnaɪt] 13 über Nacht

overnighters [əʊvəˈnaɪtəz] 2 *overnighters welcome (= Leute, die nur eine Nacht bleiben wollen, sind auf diesem RV-Platz willkommen)*

overtime [ˈəʊvətaɪm] 5/6 Überstunden; *work overtime* Überstunden machen

own [əʊn] 9/11 *they each have their own personal computer* jeder hat seinen eigenen PC; *in your own words* in Ihren eigenen Worten; *make your own paper* machen Sie sich Ihr eigenes Papier; *I've got a computer of my own* ich habe einen eigenen Computer

owners' manual [ˈəʊnəz ˈmænjʊəl] 1 Betriebsanleitung, Betriebsanweisung

oxygen [ˈɒksɪdʒən] A8/16 Sauerstoff; *oxygen-monitoring device* Sauerstoffüberwachungsanlage

ozone [ˈəʊzəʊn] 7 Ozon

P

package [ˈpækɪdʒ] 12 Paket; Packen

packaging [ˈpækɪdʒɪŋ] 11 Verpackung; Verpacken

panel [ˈpænl] A9 Paneel; *control panel* Schalttafel; *solar panel* Sonnenkollektor; Solarzellenpanel

paper input [ˈpeɪpə ˈɪnpʊt] 19 Papierzuführung

paper machine 11 Papiermaschine

papermaker [ˈpeɪpəmeɪkə] 1 Papiermacher

paper output [ˈpeɪpə ˈaʊtpʊt] 19 Papierablage

parabolic dish [pærəˈbɒlɪk] 4 Parabolantenne

parallel interface [ˈpærəlel] T2 parallele Schnittstelle

parking lot [ˈpɑːkɪŋ lɒt] 13 *(US:)* Parkplatz *(GB:* car park)

parking ticket [ˈpɑːkɪŋ ˈtɪkɪt] 13 Strafzettel für Falschparken

particle [ˈpɑːtɪkl] 11 Teilchen; Partikel

pass [pɑːs] 5/6/9/12 *pass a message on* eine Mitteilung weitergeben; *we passed a large building* wir gingen an einem großen Gebäude vorbei; *trains can pass through* Züge können durchfahren; *light can pass through* Licht kann durchscheinen; *it passes round a series of cylinders* es geht um eine Reihe von Zylindern herum

passage ['pæsɪdʒ] T1/A13 Gang; Durchgang; Durchlauf; *an underground passage* ein unterirdischer Gang

pattern ['pætən] 20 Muster

payment ['peɪmənt] 1 Bezahlung

peak times [piːk] 5 Spitzenzeiten

percentage [pə'sentɪdʒ] 4 Prozentsatz

perform [pə'fɔːm] 10 *perform an action* eine Operation durchführen

performance [pə'fɔːməns] 8 Leistung

period ['pɪərɪəd] 7/15/16 *a period of change* eine Zeit der Veränderungen; *a period of time* eine Zeitspanne; *(US:)* Punkt *(GB:* full stop)

permit [pə'mɪt] 13 erlauben

pests [pests] 14 Ungeziefer, Schädlinge

petrol ['petrəl] A14 *(GB:)* Benzin *(US:* gas/ gasoline)

petrol consumption ['petrəl kən'sʌmpʃn] 8 Benzinverbrauch

petroleum [pɪ'trəʊljəm] 6 Rohöl

pharmaceutical [fɑːmə'sjuːtɪkl] A17 pharmazeutisch

phone [fəʊn] 2 *on the phone* am Telefon

photographic [fəʊtə'græfɪk] 17 fotografisch; Foto-

photovoltaics [fəʊtəʊvɒl'teɪks] A15 Photovoltaik *(= die direkte Umsetzung von Lichtenergie in elektrische Energie mit Hilfe von Halbleitermaterialien)*

pick [pɪk] 3/5/7 *will you pick up your ticket at the airport?* werden Sie Ihren Flugschein am Flughafen abholen? *pick up power* Strom aufnehmen *I'll pick you up* ich hole Sie ab

pictorial views [pɪk'tɔːrɪəl] 3 Bilddarstellungen

pile [paɪl] 12 Stapel; Haufen

pilot light ['paɪlət] 2 *(hier:)* Zündflamme

pin [pɪn] 3/9 Stift; Pin; Nadel; *pin-ended pivots* mit Spitzen versehene Drehzapfen; *three-pin plug* dreipoliger Stecker

pipe [paɪp] 12 Rohr

piston ['pɪstən] 18/A18 Kolben

pivot ['pɪvət] 9 Drehzapfen

place [pleɪs] 11 *place the second sheet of blotting paper on top* legen Sie das zweite Blatt Löschpapier oben drauf

planet ['plænɪt] 4 Planet

plant [plɑːnt] 4/10/T1/11/12/16 Anlage; Fabrikanlage; *assembly plant* Montagewerk; *manufacturing plant* Produktionsanlage

plant [plɑːnt] 11/12 Pflanze; pflanzen

plastic ['plæstɪk] 1/7/17 Kunststoff; synthetisch; *plastic bag* Kunststofftüte, Plastikbeutel; *foam plastics* Schaumkunststoffe

plate [pleɪt] 14 Teller; Platte

platinum ['plætɪnəm] A17/T2 Platin

pliers ['plaɪəz] 1 Zange; *cutting pliers* Schneidzange

plug [plʌg] 3/5 Stecker; Stöpsel; einstecken; *three-pin plug* dreipoliger Stecker; *plug something in* anschließen *(an der Steckdose)*

plumbing ['plʌmɪŋ] 15 Wasserrohrinstallation; (die) Wasserleitungen

plus [plʌs] 12 plus

point [pɔɪnt] 7/11/13/16/18 *it's the starting point* es ist der Anfang; *I don't quite see the point* ich sehe nicht ganz, was das soll; *I take your point but…* ich sehe, was Sie meinen, aber…; *what's the point of this?* was hat das für einen Zweck? *what are the points to look for?* nach welchen Punkten sollen wir suchen?

pole [pəʊl] A13 Pol

polish ['pɒlɪʃ] 1/13 polieren; abreiben

pollutant [pə'luːtənt] A7 Schadstoff

pollute [pə'luːt] 4/7 verunreinigen; verschmutzen; *a polluted lake* ein verschmutzter See; *polluted with sewage* mit Abwasser verschmutzt

pollution [pə'luːʃn] 7 Verunreinigung; Verschmutzung; *air pollution* Luftverschmutzung; *water pollution* Wasserverschmutzung

polymeric material [pɒlɪ'merɪk] T2 Polymer

portable ['pɔːtəbl] T2 tragbar

position [pə'zɪʃn] 10 Lage; Position

pour [pɔː] 12 gießen; schütten

power ['paʊə] 1/7/8/T1/14/15 *power supply* Energieversorgung; *power drill* Motorbohrer; *power output* Ausgangsleistung; *power supply* Stromversorgung; *power failure* Stromausfall; *nuclear power* Atomkraft; *hydro-electric power* Wasserkraft; *they have the power to change the environment* sie haben die Kraft, die Umwelt zu verändern; *powered by diesel engines* von Dieselmotoren angetrieben; *power from light* Energie aus Licht

power station ['paʊə 'steɪʃn] 7 Kraftwerk; Elektrizitätswerk

prairie ['preərɪ] 6 Prärie *(= Grasland in Kanada und den USA)*

precious metal ['preʃəs] 17 Edelmetall

precipitator [prɪ'sɪpɪteɪtə] 10 Abscheider; Filter

precision [prɪ'sɪʒn] 1 Präzision; *precision instrument* Feinmeßgerät

presence ['preznz] T1 Anwesenheit

present [prɪ'zent] 15 *the hospital presents a new concept* das Krankenhaus stellt ein neues Konzept dar

press [pres] 12 pressen; (stark) drücken

press release ['pres rɪ'liːs] 17 Pressemitteilung

press roller ['pres rəʊlə] 12 Preßwalze

pressure ['preʃə] 2/10/14/16 Druck; *high-pressure steam* Hochdruckdampf; *low-pressure* Niederdruck-

pressure relief valve ['preʃə] 2 Druckbegrenzungsventil

prestressed [priː'strest] 9 vorgespannt

prevent [prɪ'vent] 15 verhindern

previous ['priːvjəs] 19 *the previous meeting* die vorherige Besprechung

principle ['prɪnsəpl] A4 Prinzip

probe [prəʊb] 4 Sonde; sondieren; erforschen; *probing the universe* (das) Erforschen des Universums

procedure [prə'siːdʒə] 3 Verfahren; *what is the regular procedure?* was ist das normale Verfahren?

process ['prəʊses] 2/10 Vorgang; Prozeß; *process engineer* Verfahrensingenieur

produce [prə'djuːs] 7/10/17/T2 produzieren; hervorbringen

product ['prɒdʌkt] 3/10 Erzeugnis; Produkt

production [prə'dʌkʃn] 8/17 Produktion; Herstellung

professional [prə'feʃnl] 11 Berufs-; *professional training* Fachausbildung

profit ['prɒfɪt] 4 *profit from something* aus etwas Gewinn ziehen

prohibit [prə'hɪbɪt] 13 verbieten

project ['prɒdʒekt] 3 Projekt; Plan

projection [prə'dʒekʃn] 3 Projektion; Ansicht, Ansichtszeichnung; Riß

promise ['prɒmɪs] 9/16 Versprechen; versprechen; *a promising anti-corrosion paint* eine vielversprechende Korrosionsschutzfarbe

proposal [prə'pəʊzl] 3/5 Vorschlag

protective cover [prə'tektɪv] A19 Schutzhülle; Schutzumschlag

protein ['prəʊtiːn] 14 Protein (= Eiweiß)

prototype ['prəʊtəʊtaɪp] A3 Prototyp

prove [pruːv] A4/T2 beweisen; nachweisen; sich erweisen (als); *it proved to be the most efficient* es stellte sich als das leistungsfähigste heraus

provide [prə'vaɪd] 9/15/16 besorgen; sorgen für; bereitstellen; *utilities are provided* Energie- und Wasserversorgung wird bereitgestellt; *we will provide the experts* wir werden für die Fachleute sorgen; *software will be provided* Software wird bereitgestellt

public ['pʌblɪk] 8/16 Öffentlichkeit; öffentlich; *public transportation* öffentliche Verkehrsmittel

publication [pʌblɪ'keɪʃn] A11 Veröffentlichung; Publikation

publish ['pʌblɪʃ] 2 veröffentlichen; publizieren

pull handle [pʊl] 16 Zuggriff

pulp [pʌlp] 11 Zellstoff *(für die Papierherstellung)*

pulp mill [pʌlp] 11 Zellstofffabrik

pump [pʌmp] 6/9 Pumpe; pumpen

pump rod [pʌmp] 6 Kolbenstange *(der Pumpe)*

punctual [ˈpʌŋktjʊəl] 12 pünktlich

punctuation [pʌŋktjʊˈeɪʃn] 16 Interpunktion; Zeichensetzung

purify [ˈpjʊərɪfaɪ] A17 reinigen

purification [pjʊərɪfɪˈkeɪʃn] T2 Reinigung

put [pʊt] 20/T2 *he put me in contact with a company* er verschaffte mir den Kontakt zu einer Firma; *I'll put you through (Telefon:)* ich verbinde Sie; *put into practice* in die Praxis umsetzen

Q

quality assurance [ˈkwɒlətɪ əˈʃʊərəns] A1 Qualitätssicherung

qualities [ˈkwɒlətɪz] 14 Eigenschaften

quantity [ˈkwɒntətɪ] 12 Menge; Quantität

quench [kwentʃ] 10 löschen; quenschen; *quensch column* Löschanlage; *quench water tank* Löschwassertank

R

radiate [ˈreɪdɪeɪt] 15 strahlen; ausstrahlen; *radiating from the core* strahlenförmig von der Mitte ausgehend

radiation [ˈreɪdɪˈeɪʃn] A8 Strahlung

radii → radius

radio-controlled [ˈreɪdɪəʊ-kənˈtrəʊld] 14 funkgesteuert

radius [ˈreɪdjəs] *(Mehrzahl:)* radii [ˈreɪdɪaɪ] 3 Radius, Halbmesser

rail [reɪl] 5/A13 Schiene; *rail tunnel* Eisenbahntunnel

range [reɪndʒ] 4/16 *our range of products* unsere Produktpalette; *within a narrow range* innerhalb einer engen Bandbreite; *a wide range of finishes* eine breite Palette von Anstrichfarben; *answers ranging from none to lots* Antworten, die sich von „keine" bis „eine Menge" erstrecken

rank [ræŋk] 12 *they always ranked first* sie standen immer in der ersten Reihe

rare [reə] A17 selten; rar

rated speed [ˈreɪtɪd] 18 Nenngeschwindigkeit

raw material [rɔ:] 8 Rohstoff

react [rɪˈækt] 2 reagieren

realistic [rɪəˈlɪstɪk] 2 realistisch

realize [ˈrɪəlaɪz] A14/A17 bemerken; erkennen; *I never realized how important this is* mir war nie klar, wie wichtig das ist; *I didn't realize* ich habe es nicht bemerkt; *when you realize…* wenn Sie sich darüber im klaren sind…

rear [rɪə] 12 hinterer Teil; hinten; *at the rear* hinten; *in the rear of…* im hinteren Teil von…

receive [rɪˈsi:v] 4/10 empfangen; bekommen; erhalten; *receive a broadcast* eine Sendung empfangen; *we received the spare parts last week* wir haben die Ersatzteile vorige Woche erhalten

receiver [rɪˈsi:və] 4 Empfänger

reception [rɪˈsepʃn] 6 Empfang

receptionist [rɪˈsepʃənɪst] 6 *(Firma:)* Empfang; Empfangssekretärin; *(Hotel:)* Empfang; Empfangschef/Empfangsdame; *(Arzt:)* Sprechstundenhilfe

recover [rɪˈkʌvə] 7 zurückgewinnen

recovery [rɪˈkʌvərɪ] 17 *the recovery of precious metals* die Zurückgewinnung von Edelmetallen

rectangle [ˈrektæŋgl] A20 Rechteck

recycle [ri:ˈsaɪkl] 7/12/17 wiederverwerten; wiederaufbereiten

recycling [ri:ˈsaɪklɪŋ] 12/17 Recycling, Wiederverwertung

reduce [rɪˈdju:s] 7/12/16 reduzieren; verringern

reduction [rɪˈdʌkʃn] 4/16 Reduzierung; Verringerung

reel [ri:l] 12 Spule; Rolle; *reel something up* etwas aufwickeln; *reel up* (die) Aufwicklung

reference [ˈrefrəns] 16 *your ref (= reference)* Ihr Zeichen

refill [ri:ˈfɪl] 2 nachfüllen; auffüllen

refine [rɪˈfaɪn] 11/17 raffinieren; veredeln; läutern; *refined pulp* veredelter Zellstoff; *refined zinc* Feinzink

refiner [rɪˈfaɪnə] 11 Refiner

refinery [rɪˈfaɪnərɪ] 17 Raffinerie; Affinerie *(zur Gold- und Silberscheidung)*

reflect [rɪˈflekt] 9 widerspiegeln

reforest [riːˈfɒrɪst] 11 aufforsten

refrigeration [rɪfrɪdʒəˈreɪʃn] 7 Kühlung

refrigerator [rɪˈfrɪdʒəreɪtə] *(Kurzform:* fridge [frɪdʒ]) 2 Kühlschrank

refuel [riːˈfjʊəl] 2 auftanken

refuse [rɪˈfjuːz] 9 ablehnen; sich weigern; *refuse an offer* ein Angebot ablehnen

region [ˈriːdʒən] 4 Gebiet; Region

regret [rɪˈgret] 19 Bedauern; bedauern; *I regret this very much* ich bedaure das sehr

regulation [regjʊˈleɪʃn] 5 Bestimmung; Vorschrift

regulator [ˈregjʊleɪtə] 2 Regler

reinforce [riːɪnˈfɔːs] 8/9/15 verstärken; *reinforced concrete* Stahlbeton

reject [rɪˈdʒekt] 5 ablehnen

relatively [ˈrelətɪvlɪ] 14 verhältnismäßig; relativ

release [rɪˈliːs] T1 freigeben; losmachen; loslassen

reliable [rɪˈlaɪəbl] zuverlässig

remarkable [rɪˈmɑːkəbl] bemerkenswert

remove [rɪˈmuːv] 11 entfernen

renewable [rɪˈnjuːəbl] 12 *renewable energy* erneuerbare Energie

rental company [ˈrentl] 2 Verleihfirma

replace [rɪˈpleɪs] 2/16 ersetzen; *it is replaced by…* es wird ersetzt durch…

report [rɪˈpɔːt] 1 Bericht; berichten

represent [reprɪˈzent] 3 darstellen; verkörpern; *it represents a break* es stellt eine Bruchkante dar

request [rɪˈkwest] 16 Bitte; Wunsch

require [rɪˈkwaɪə] 10/12/T2 *it requires large quantities of clean water* es erfordert große Mengen sauberes Wasser; *the steam required* der erforderliche Dampf; *if required* wenn erforderlich; *required by law* gesetzlich vorgeschrieben

requirements [rɪˈkwaɪəmənts] A17 Bedarf, Erfordernisse; *meet the requirements* den Bedarf decken

research [rɪˈsɜːtʃ] 8/14 Forschung; forschen; *…are being researched* werden gerade erforscht

reserve [rɪˈzɜːv] 3/18 Reserve; reservieren

reservoir [ˈrezəvwaː] 14 Reservoir; Speicher; Behälter

resident parking [ˈrezɪdənt] 17 Parken nur für Anwohner

residential area [rezɪˈdenʃl] 16 Wohngebiet

residue [ˈrezɪdjuː] 10 Rückstand; Rest

respectively [rɪˈspektɪvlɪ] 20 beziehungsweise

response [rɪˈspɒns] 20 Antwort; Reaktion

rest [rest] 15 *it rests on steel beams* es ruht auf Stahlträgern

restrict [rɪˈstrɪkt] 20 einschränken; beschränken

restriction [rɪˈstrɪkʃn] 13 Einschränkung; Beschränkung

result [rɪˈzʌlt] 2/11/15 Ergebnis; Resultat; Folge; zu etwas führen; zur Folge haben; *that can result in problems* das kann zu Problemen führen; *the studies resulted in a new structure* die Studien hatten eine neue Struktur zur Folge; *the result of the studies* das Ergebnis der Studien

retraining centre [riːˈtreɪnɪŋ] 14 Umschulungszentrum

reusable [riːˈjuːzəbl] 12 wiederverwendbar

rid [rɪd] 7 *get rid of garbage* den Müll loswerden

ride [raɪd] 5/T1/13 *take a ride* eine Fahrt machen; *ride a bicycle* Fahrrad fahren; *ride a motor bike* Motorrad fahren

right [raɪt] 8/15 *right up to London* bis nach London hoch; *right to the centre* direkt bis ins Zentrum

ring [rɪŋ] 11 *the phone was ringing* das Telefon klingelte

rise [raɪz] (rose [rəʊz] – have risen [ˈrɪzn]) aufsteigen; in die Höhe gehen; *a vertical shaft rises from the centre of the base* eine senkrechte Säule geht vom Zentrum des Fundaments hoch; *when the sun rises* wenn die Sonne aufgeht; *this mountain rises to 2,500 metres* dieser Berg ragt 2500 Meter hoch

risk [rɪsk] 5 Risiko; riskieren

rivet ['rɪvɪt] 1 Niete

robot ['rəʊbɒt] 1 Roboter

rockfall ['rɒkfɔ:l] T1 Steinschlag

rocky ['rɒkɪ] 6 felsig

rod [rɒd] 6/12 Stange; Gestänge; Stab

roller ['rəʊlə] 12 Walze; Rolle

root [ru:t] 12 Wurzel

rope [rəʊp] A9 Seil; Tau; Kabel

rotate [rəʊ'teɪt] 10/16/A19 (sich) drehen; rotieren

rough [rʌf] 1 rauh; uneben; grob

routine [ru:'ti:n] A8 Routine

row [rəʊ] 14 Reihe; *in straight rows* in geraden Reihen

rubber ['rʌbə] A12 Gummi

run [rʌn] (ran [ræn] – have run) A1/2/5/T1 13/14/T2 *run a program* ein Programm durchlaufen lassen; *a running engine* ein laufender Motor; *the conveyor belt was running* das Förderband lief/war in Betrieb; *they will be run by computers* sie werden von Computern gesteuert; *we've run out of spare parts* wir haben keine Ersatzteile mehr; *these cars run on petrol* diese Autos fahren mit Benzin; *it runs on batteries* es läuft auf Batterie

rust [rʌst] T2 Rost; rosten

RV ['ɑ: 'vi:] (= recreational vehicle [rekrɪ'eɪʃnl 'vi:ɪkl] 2 Freizeitfahrzeug *(z. B. Reisemobil, Wohnmobil, Kastenwagen etc.)*

S

safety precautions [prɪ'kɔ:ʃnz] 5 Sicherheitsvorkehrungen

salutation [sælju:'teɪʃn] 16 *(Brief:)* Grußformel

satellite ['sætəlaɪt] 4 Satellit

satisfied ['sætɪsfaɪd] 16/19 zufrieden

saw [sɔ:] 1 Säge; sägen

scalable fonts ['skeɪləbl 'fɒnts] 19 skalierbare Schriften

scale [skeɪl] 3/8/10 *what scale is used for this drawing?* welcher Maßstab wird für diese Zeichnung verwendet? *large-scale experiments* Großversuche; *on a large scale* in großem Umfang; *scale 1:1* (im) Maßstab 1:1

scan [skæn] 19 abtasten; absuchen

scanner ['skænə] 19 Scanner; Abtaster

scatter ['skætə] T1 verstreuen; *...are scattered over the diggings* ...sind über die Abbaustellen verstreut

schedule ['ʃedju:l / *US auch:* 'skedju:l] 9/14 Tabelle; Zeitplan; Fahrplan; Programm; *on schedule* planmäßig; *train schedule* Zugfahrplan

science ['saɪəns] 13 Wissenschaft

scientist ['saɪəntɪst] 4 Wissenschaftler(in)

scissors ['sɪzəz] A3 Schere

Scotch tape ['skɒtʃ 'teɪp] 3 *(US:)* Tesafilm *(GB:* sellotape ['seləʊteɪp])

screen [skri:n] 3/7 Bildschirm; Leinwand; Schutzschirm

screw [skru:] 1 Schraube *(ohne Mutter)*

screwdriver ['skru:draɪvə] 1 Schraubendreher

sea-sickness ['si:sɪknɪs] 5 Seekrankheit

second growth forest [:sekənd grəʊθ 'fɒrɪst] 11 nachgewachsener Wald

section ['sekʃn] 3/10/14 Stück; Teil; Abteilung; Sektion; *to section lines* Schnitt zeichnen; *sectioning* Schnittzeichnen; *bolts are sectioned* Schrauben werden im Schnitt dargestellt; *crooked sections* krumme Teile

sector ['sektə] 8 Bereich; Sektor

security system [sɪ'kjʊərətɪ 'sɪstɪm] A7/15 Sicherheitssystem

seek [si:k] (sought [sɔ:t] – have sought) A16/16 suchen; *seek advice* Rat suchen; *seek a solution* eine Lösung suchen

see [si:] (saw [sɔ:] – have seen [si:n]) 14 *I'll have it seen to immediately* ich werde dafür sorgen, daß sich sofort jemand darum kümmert

sellotape ['seləʊteɪp] *(GB:)* Tesafilm *(US:* Scotch tape ['skɒtʃ 'teɪp])

semi-finished ['semɪ'fɪnɪʃt] A17 *semi-finished products* Halbfertigprodukte

senior citizens ['si:njə] 12 ältere Bürger(innen), Senioren/Seniorinnen

sensor ['sensə] 8 Sensor; Fühler

separate ['sepəreɪt] 7 *separate the garbage* den Abfall trennen (= sortieren); *oil separator* Ölabscheider

sequence ['siːkwəns] 20 Reihenfolge; (logische) Abfolge

serial interface ['sɪərɪəl 'ɪntəfeɪs] T2 serielle Schnittstelle

service ['sɜːvɪs] 5/8/10/13/15 *service train* Reparatur- und Wartungszug; *service technician* Servicetechniker; *I was glad to be of service* ich war froh, daß ich Ihnen helfen konnte; *the car is being serviced* der Wagen wird gerade gemacht (= Kundendienstservice); *the steam trains are not in service* die Dampfeisenbahn ist nicht in Betrieb; *service elevator (etwa:)* Lastenaufzug; *service life* Lebensdauer

set [set] A1/1 Satz; Serie; Set; *a set of data* eine Reihe von Daten

set up [set] 4/13 *set up a distribution system* ein Verteilersystem aufbauen; *the whole set-up* die ganze Anordnung, der gesamte Aufbau

settler ['setlə] 14 Siedler

sewage ['sjuːɪdʒ] 4/7 Abwasser; *sewage treatment* Abwasserreinigung

shaft [ʃɑːft] 3/T1/15 Welle; Schacht; *drive shaft* Antriebswelle

shake [ʃeɪk] (shook [ʃʊk] – have shaken ['ʃeɪkn]) 12 Schütteln; schütteln; *he shook his head* er schüttelte den Kopf

shape [ʃeɪp] 15 Form; formen; *the right shape* die richtige Form; *in the shape of a cross* in der Form eines Kreuzes; *cross-shaped* kreuzförmig

sharp [ʃɑːp] 13/T2 *a sharp knife* ein scharfes Messer; *at six o'clock sharp* pünktlich um sechs; *a sharp increase* eine kräftige Steigerung

sharpen ['ʃɑːpən] 1 schärfen

shave [ʃeɪv] 3 *electric shaver* Elektrorasierer

sheet [ʃiːt] 11 *a sheet of paper* ein Blatt Papier; *sheet steel* Stahlblech; *sheet-metal screw* Blechschraube; *sheet metal* Blech

shield [ʃiːld] 7 (Schutz-)Schild

shift [ʃɪft] 5 *shift work* Schichtarbeit; *have you ever worked in shifts?* haben Sie jemals Schichtarbeit gemacht? *night shift* Nachtschicht

shoot movies [ʃuːt] (shot [ʃɒt] – have shot) 14 Filme drehen

shop floor ['ʃɒp 'flɔː] 20 Produktionsstätte; *the shop floor* die Arbeiter, die Belegschaft; *the worker on the shop floor* der „einfache" Arbeiter

shower ['ʃaʊə] 2 Dusche

shut-down ['ʃʌtdaʊn] 10 Schließung; Abschaltung

shutter ['ʃʌtə] A5 Rollgitter; (Fenster-)Laden; Verschluß; Rolladen

shuttle ['ʃʌtl] 5 *passenger shuttle* Passagierpendelverkehr

silica ['sɪlɪkə] A17 Siliziumdioxid; *silica glass* Quarzglas

silicate ['sɪlɪkɪt] A17 Silikat

silk [sɪlk] 12 Seide

silver ['sɪlvə] 17 Silber

simplify ['sɪmplɪfaɪ] 9 vereinfachen

sincerely [sɪn'sɪəlɪ] 16 *yours sincerely (Briefformel:)* mit freundlichen Grüßen

sink drainer [sɪŋk] 2 Spülbeckenabfluß

site [saɪt] 5/9 *construction site/building site* Baustelle; *it's located on a site...* es befindet sich auf einem Gelände...

sketch [sketʃ] 3 Skizze; *make a sketch* eine Skizze anfertigen

skyscaper ['skaɪskreɪpə] 5 Wolkenkratzer

slate [sleɪt] 14 Schiefer

slightly ['slaɪtlɪ] 9 geringfügig

soak [səʊk] 11 einweichen; durchtränken

soccer ['sɒkə] A9 Fußball

socket ['sɒkɪt] 9 *steel sockets* Stahlbuchsen; *a plug and a socket* ein Stecker und eine Steckdose; *socket wrench* Steckschlüssel; *socketed strand* Kabel mit Buchse

software ['sɒftweə] A1 Software (= *Sammelbegriff für alle nichtapparativen Funktionsbestandteile bei der elektronischen Datenverarbeitung, z. B. Betriebssysteme und Programme*)

solar ['səʊlə] 4/8/9/14/A15 Sonnen-

solid ['sɒlɪd] 3 *solid parts*; Feststoffe

solution [sə'lu:ʃn] 7/12 Lösung *(auch chemisch)*

solve [sɒlv] 4 *solve a problem* ein Problem lösen

sophisticated [sə'fɪstɪkeɪtɪd] 7 hochentwickelt; hochtechnisiert

source [sɔ:s] 7/12/16/17 Quelle

space [speɪs] 4/5/9/11/15 Raum; *satellites in space* Satelliten im Weltraum; *open spaces* offene Flächen

span [spæn] 5 *bridge span* Brückenspannweite

spanner ['spænə] 1 *(GB:)* Schraubenschlüssel *(US:* wrench)

spare parts ['speə 'pɑːts] A9/10 Ersatzteile

spark plug ['spɑːk plʌg] *(GB auch:* sparking plug) 15 Zündkerze

species ['spiːʃiːz] 11 Art; Spezies

specifications [spesɪfɪ'keɪʃnz] 1 technische Daten

spell [spel] 20 buchstabieren

spin [spɪn] 13 sich schnell drehen; schleudern

spray [spreɪ] 14/18 spritzen; (be)sprühen

spray-paint ['spreɪ-peɪnt] 8 spritzlackieren

spring [sprɪŋ] 9 Feder

squeeze [skwiːz] 12 ausdrücken; drücken; quetschen

stadium ['steɪdjəm] 9 Stadion

staff [stɑːf] A13 Mitarbeiter; Belegschaft

stage [steɪdʒ] 10 Stufe

stainless steel ['steɪnlɪs 'stiːl] A13 nichtrostender Stahl

standard ['stændəd] 3 Norm; Maßstab; *safety standards* Sicherheitsnormen; *drawing standards* Zeichennormen

starch [stɑːtʃ] 11 Stärke *(= Material zum Steifen und Kleben)*

start [stɑːt] 10 *easy to start up* leicht in Betrieb zu setzen

starter ['stɑːtə] 5 Anlasser

statement ['steɪtmənt] A3 Feststellung; Behauptung

statistics [stə'tɪstɪks] A20 Statistik(en)

stay [steɪ] 17 *stay ahead of the competition* der Konkurrenz voraus bleiben

steel [stiːl] 1/9 Stahl

steep [stiːp] 14 steil

steer [stɪə] 5/A18 steuern; lenken

steering ['stɪərɪŋ] 5 Lenkung; Steuerung

step [step] 9/11/A13/13 *step on the rail* auf die Schiene treten; *the first steps* die ersten Schritte; *step off the escalator* von der Rolltreppe heruntergehen

stock [stɒk] 12 *have something in stock* etwas auf Lager haben

stockholders ['stɒkhəʊldəz] A17 Aktionäre

stopper ['stɒpə] A13 Verschluß; Korken

storage ['stɔːrɪdʒ] 2 Lagerung; Speicherung

store ['stɔː] 14 lagern; speichern

storey ['stɔːrɪ] 15 *two-storey base* zweistöckiges Fundament

straight [streɪt] T1/A4/11 *straight sides* gerade Seiten; *in straight lines* in geraden Linien; *straight from London* direkt aus London; *go straight on* geradeaus gehen

strand [strænd] 9/A16 Strang; Litze

stress loadings ['stres 'ləʊdɪŋz] 9 Spannungsbelastungen

stretch [stretʃ] 12 strecken; dehnen

string [strɪŋ] A13 Kordel

strip [strɪp] 3/11 *paper strip* Papierstreifen; *Möbius strip* Möbiusstreifen; *the bark is stripped from the logs* die Rinde wird von den Baumstämmen entfernt; *strip trees* Bäume entrinden

stripe [straɪp] 6 Streifen; *magnetic stripe* Magnetstreifen

structural steel ['strʌktʃərəl] 9 Baustahl

structural system ['strʌktʃərəl] 15 Konstruktionssystem

structure ['strʌktʃə] 8 Struktur; Bau; Bauweise

subject [səb'dʒekt] A8/9 *it was subjected to different stress loadings* es wurde verschiedenen Spannungsbelastungen ausgesetzt; *subject to tyre limitations* abhängig von den Reifenbelastungsgrenzen

subject line ['sʌbdʒɪkt] 16 *(Brief:)* Betrifft

substance ['sʌbstəns] 7 Substanz; Material

subway [ˈsʌbweɪ] A13 *(US:)* Untergrundbahn; *(GB:)* Fußgängerunterführung

suction box [ˈsʌkʃn] 12 Saugkasten; Sauger

suffer [ˈsʌfə] A7 *suffer from something* unter/ an etwas leiden; *this project suffers from bad planning* dieses Projekt leidet unter der schlechten Planung

sulphur *(auch:* sulfur) [ˈsʌlfə] 10 Schwefel

sum [sʌm] 9/20 *a large sum* eine große Summe; *sum up something* etwas zusammenfassen

supplier [səˈplaɪə] 7 Lieferant(in)

supplies [səˈplaɪz] A9 Vorräte; Lieferungen

supply [səˈplaɪ] 9/16 liefern; zuführen; *they supply the steel* sie liefern den Stahl; *these parts are supplied by us* diese Teile werden von uns geliefert

supply valve [səˈplaɪ] 2 Speiseventil; Zuleitungsventil

support [səˈpɔːt] 9 stützen; unterstützen

support cable [səˈpɔːt] 9 Tragseil

support system [səˈpɔːt] 9 Tragesystem

surface [ˈsɜːfɪs] 1 Oberfläche

survey [ˈsɜːveɪ] 7 *a telephone survey* eine Telefonbefragung; *conduct a survey* eine Umfrage durchführen; *survey of land* Landvermessung; *a survey of the situation* eine Übersicht über die Lage

survive [səˈvaɪv] 13 überleben

switch [swɪtʃ] 1/2/7/14/16 *switch the machine on* die Maschine anschalten; *switch off* abschalten; *they will switch to nuclear energy* sie werden (sich) auf Atomenergie umstellen; *we're switching over to plastics* wir stellen (uns) auf Kunststoff um; *where is the switch?* wo ist der Schalter? *the switch to new products* die Umstellung auf neue Produkte

switchboard [ˈswɪtʃbɔːd] 20 Telefonzentrale; Vermittlung

symbol [ˈsɪmbl] 3 Symbol

synthetic [sɪnˈθetɪk] A17 synthetisch

T

table saw [ˈteɪbl sɔː] 1 Tisch(kreis)säge

tag [tæg] A8/19 *tag axle* Mittelachse; *tag question* Frageanhängsel

tailpipe [ˈteɪlpaɪp] A17 Endrohr *(= Auspuffrohr)*

take [teɪk] (took [tʊk] – have taken [ˈteɪkn]) 1/ 2/7/12/14/17/18/20 *take notes* Notizen machen; *is this seat taken?* ist dieser Platz besetzt? *take over a company* eine Firma übernehmen; *jobs have been taken over by machines* Arbeitsplätze sind von Maschinen übernommen worden; *take part in a meeting* an einer Sitzung teilnehmen; *take a ride on one of the service trains* mit einem der Servicezüge fahren; *take the first step* den ersten Schritt tun; *this has been taken into account* das ist berücksichtigt worden; *take responsibility* Verantwortung übernehmen; *I take your point* ich verstehe, was Sie meinen; *take care of room repairs* sich um die Zimmerreparaturen kümmern; *take sides* Partei ergreifen; *can I take a message?* kann ich etwas ausrichten? *it would have taken me a lot of time* das hätte mich eine Menge Zeit gekostet; *this engine has taken five years to develop* es hat fünf Jahre gedauert, diesen Motor zu entwickeln; *everyone has taken this for granted* jeder hat das als selbstverständlich hingenommen

tar [tɑː] 10 Teer

target [ˈtɑːgɪt] 5 Ziel

tear [ˈteə] (tore [tɔː] – have torn [tɔːn]) 11 reißen; abreißen; zerreißen; *tear something open* etwas aufreißen; *tear something to pieces* etwas in Stücke reißen; *tear something in half* etwas entzweireißen, etwas zerreißen

technical [ˈteknɪkəl] 1/3/9 technisch; *a technical problem* ein technisches Problem; *technically speaking* technisch gesprochen; *technical draughtsman (US:* draftsman*)* technischer Zeichner/technische Zeichnerin

technician [tekˈnɪʃn] 1/5 Techniker(in)

technique [tekˈniːk] 17 Technik *(= Methode, technisches Verfahren)*

technological [teknə'lɒdʒɪkl] 3 technologisch; technisch

technology [tek'nɒlədʒɪ] 7/8 Technologie

telecommunications ['telɪkəmjuːnɪ'keɪʃnz] T2 Fernmeldewesen

telescope ['telɪskəʊp] 4 Fernrohr; Teleskop

temperature ['temprətʃə] T2/10 Temperatur

temporary ['tempərərɪ] 5 vorübergehend; temporär

tend [tend] 11 *tend forests* sich um Wälder kümmern

terminal ['tɜːmɪnl] 5/13 Terminal; Endstation; Bahnhof

thermal ['θɜːml] 9/10 thermisch; Wärme-; *thermal insulation* Wärmeisolierung; *thermal efficiency* Wärmewirkungsgrad

thermometer [θə'mɒmɪtə] 7 Thermometer

thickness ['θɪknɪs] 12 Dicke

thorough ['θʌrə] 6/15/17 gründlich; *they are cleaned thoroughly* sie werden gründlich gereinigt

thread [θred] 3 Gewinde

threat [θret] 7 Bedrohung; Drohung

three-way catalyst ['θriː-weɪ] 16 Dreiwegekatalysator

through [θruː] 10/11/12 *through gradually increasing temperature zones* durch allmählich ansteigende Temperaturzonen; *it flows through channels* es fließt durch Kanäle; *through rollers* durch Walzen

throughout [θruː'aʊt] 10/T2 *repainted throughout* von oben bis unten neu gestrichen; *throughout the world* in der ganzen Welt

thus [ðʌs] A4 so; dadurch; damit

ticket office ['tɪkɪt] 13 Kartenschalter

tiedown ['taɪdaʊn] 9 Verankerung

tightly drawn ['taɪtlɪ] A13 fest gespannt

tilt [tɪlt] 11 kippen; neigen

time [taɪm] 7/10/T1/16 *on time* pünktlich; *just in time* gerade noch rechtzeitig; *it might be time for a change* vielleicht ist es Zeit für einen Wechsel; *30 times as much* dreißig Mal so viel

timekeeper ['taɪmkiːpə] A5 Zeitnehmer(in)

timetable ['taɪmteɪbl] 6 Stundenplan; Zeitplan; Fahrplan

tire *(US)* ['taɪə] *(GB:* tyre) A12 Reifen

tissue ['tɪʃuː] A11 *(hier:)* Papiertaschentuch; *(auch:)* Gewebe

toilet ['tɔɪlɪt] 2 Toilette

tolerance ['tɒlərəns] 17 Toleranz

ton/tonne [tʌn] A9 ton = englische und amerikanische Tonne; *tonne* = metrische Tonne

toner ['təʊnə] 19 Toner *(z. B. für Kopierer oder Drucker)*

tool-path ['tuːl-pɑːθ] 20 Werkzeug-Verfahrweg *(= numerische Steuerung)*

toolmaker ['tuːlmeɪkə] 1 Werkzeugmacher

tooth [tuːθ] *(Mehrzahl:* teeth [tiːθ]) 13 Zahn *(auch eines Zahnrades)*

top [tɒp] 11/16 *on top* oben; *top speed* Spitzengeschwindigkeit

top gas ['tɒp gæs] 10 Destillatgas

tough [tʌf] 12/18 fest; hart; zäh; *as tough as leather* zäh wie Leder; *we had a tough time* wir hatten eine schwere Zeit; *a tough job* eine harte Arbeit; *a tough material* ein widerstandsfähiges Material

toy (tɔɪ) A13 Spielzeug

tracks [træks] T1/A13 Schienen; Fahrspuren; Spuren

tractor ['træktə] 18 Traktor

traditional [trə'dɪʃnl] 17 traditionell

trail [treɪl] 13 Pfad; Spur; Fährte

trailbikes ['treɪlbaɪks] 13 Trailbikes *(= leichte, geländegängige Motorräder)*

trainee [treɪ'niː] 1 Trainee; Praktikant(in)

transfer station ['trænsfɜː] 19 *(Laserdrucker:)* Transfereinheit

transform [træns'fɔːm] 12 umwandeln; verwandeln; transformieren; *transform heat into energy* Wärme in Energie umwandeln

transformer [træns'fɔːmə] 16 Transformator

transmission [trænz'mɪʃn] 4/6 *international transmissions* internationale Sendungen; *automatic transmission* Automatikgetriebe

transmit [trænz'mɪt] 4/13 übertragen

transparent [træns'pærent] A4 transparent

trash (US) [træʃ] 7 Abfall; *trash can* Abfall-eimer; *trash man* Müllmann; *trash bin* Abfalleimer

treat [triːt] 10 behandeln

treatment ['triːtmənt] 7/11 Behandlung

tropical ['trɒpɪkl] 12 tropisch

troubleshooter ['trʌblʃuːtə] 10 Troubleshooter *(= jemand, der Störungen oder Probleme finden und beseitigen soll)*

trunk call [trʌŋk] 20 (GB:) Ferngespräch; (US: long-distance call)

tub [tʌb] 12 Kübel; Bütte

tunnel ['tʌnl] 3/5 Tunnel

turbine ['tɜːbaɪn] 11 Turbine

turn [tɜːn] 1/6/8/9/11/13/16/17 drehen; Drehung; *let's turn off here* laß uns hier abbiegen; *in turn* einer nach dem anderen; *it's turned into a number of different products* es wird in eine Reihe von unterschiedlichen Produkten verwandelt; *turn the machine off* schalten Sie die Maschine aus/ab; *wheel B will turn twice as fast* Rad B wird sich zweimal so schnell drehen; *we must turn it upside down* wir müssen es auf den Kopf stellen (herumdrehen); *turn water into steam* Wasser in Dampf verwandeln; *turn down the air conditioning* die Klimaanlage herunterdrehen

turning circle ['tɜːnɪŋ] A8 Wendekreis

twist [twɪst] 3 drehen; verdrehen; *a full twist* eine ganze Drehung; *a twisted band* ein gedrehtes Band

tyre (GB) ['taɪə] (US: tire) A8 Reifen

U

unaccompanied [ʌnə'kʌmpənɪd] 4 unbegleitet

under separate cover ['ʌndə] 2 mit getrennter Post

underside ['ʌndəsaɪd] 18 Unterseite

unemployed ['ʌnɪm'plɔɪd] 15 arbeitslos

unemployment ['ʌnɪm'plɔɪmənt] 20 Arbeitslosigkeit

unfortunately [ʌn'fɔːtʃnətlɪ] 12 leider; unglücklicherweise

unique [juː'niːk] 10 einzigartig

unit ['juːnɪt] 16 Einheit

unlevel [ʌn'levl] 2 *if the vehicle is unlevel* wenn das Fahrzeug nicht gerade steht

unthinkable [ʌn'θɪŋkəbl] 11 undenkbar

up [ʌp] 5/8/T1 *up to 200 cars* bis zu 200 Autos; *meet up under the Channel* (sich) unter dem Kanal treffen (= aufeinanderstoßen); *up there* da oben; *right up to London* direkt bis London

uphill ['ʌp'hɪl] 2 *on the uphill side* auf der bergauf führenden Seite

upper deck ['ʌpə] 9 oberes Stockwerk; oberes Deck

upside down ['ʌpsaɪd 'daʊn] 11 verkehrt herum; umgekehrt

uranium [ju'reɪnjəm] T1 Uran

utility [juː'tɪlətɪ] 15 *of great utility* von großem Nutzen; *public utility* öffentlicher Versorgungsbetrieb; *utilities* Hausanschlüsse *(= Gas, Wasser, Strom)*

utilize ['juːtɪlaɪz] 8/15 nutzen; verwenden

V

vacation [və'keɪʃn] 2 (US:) Ferien (GB: holiday)

vacuum ['vækjʊəm] A11 Vakuum; *vacuum cleaner* Staubsauger

valuable ['væljʊəbl] 2 wertvoll

valve [vælv] (hier:) Ventil; (auch:) Röhre

van [væn] 8 Lieferwagen

van conversion ['væn kən'vɜːʃn] 2 Wohnwagen *(= ausgebauter Kastenwagen)*

vapour ['veɪpə] 10/16 Dampf

variety [və'raɪətɪ] 11 *a great variety of things* eine Vielzahl von Dingen

various ['veərɪəs] A19 verschieden

vary ['veərɪ] 16/18 variieren; schwanken

vast]vaːst] 12 enorm groß; riesig

vat [væt] 11/12 Kübel; Bütte

vehicle ['viːɪkl] 2/5/8/T1 Fahrzeug

ventilate ['ventɪleɪt] 5 belüften; lüften

ventilation [ventɪ'leɪʃn] 5 Belüftung; Lüftung

vertical ['vɜːtɪkl] 15 senkrecht; vertikal

via ['vaɪə] 8/16 *transport via tankers* Transport durch Tanker; *via air mail* mit Luftpost

vibration [vaɪˈbreɪʃn] 18 Schwingung; Vibration

vice [vaɪs] 1 Schraubstock

virus [ˈvaɪərəs] T2 Virus

visual [ˈvɪzjʊəl] 10 visuell; Sicht-

volatile matter [ˈvɒlətaɪl] 10 flüchtige Stoffe

voltage [ˈvəʊltɪdʒ] 7 (elektrische) Spannung; *high voltage* Hochspannung

voluntarily [ˈvɒləntərɪlɪ] 12 freiwillig

W

wage [weɪdʒ] 13 *hourly wage* Stundenlohn

waggon [ˈwægən] 5 Waggon

wallpaper [ˈwɔːlpeɪpə] A11 Tapete

wardrobe [ˈwɔːdrəʊb] 2 Kleiderschrank

warranty [ˈwɒrəntɪ] T2 Garantie

washer [ˈwɒʃə] 3 Dichtungsscheibe

waste [weɪst] 7/11/12/14/17 Abfall; verschwenden; *waste from the kitchen* Küchenabfälle; *waste water* Abwasser; *waste wood* Abfallholz; *don't waste energy* verschwenden Sie keine Energie

water jacket [ˈwɔːtə ˈdʒækɪt] 10 Wasserkühlmantel

water purifier [ˈwɔːtə ˈpjʊərɪfaɪə] T2 Wasserreinigungsanlage

watertight [ˈwɔːtətaɪt] 20 wasserdicht

waterway [ˈwɔːtəweɪ] 5 Wasserstraße

wave [weɪv] 4/15 Welle

way [weɪ] 1/3/7/16 *which way will the big wheel turn?* in welche Richtung wird sich das große Rad drehen? *a one-way ticket* eine einfache Fahrkarte/ein einfacher Flugschein (= nicht hin und zurück); *can I help you in any way?* kann ich Ihnen irgendwie helfen?

wear [weə] (wore [wɔː] – have worn [wɔːn]) 4/8/11 *hard hats must be worn* Helme müssen getragen werden; *I didn't wear a hard hat* ich hatte keinen Helm auf; *the pistons are worn out* die Kolben sind abgenutzt

weed [wiːd] 14 Unkraut

weld [weld] 8 schweißen; *welding* (die) Schweißung

well [wel] 6 Quelle; Brunnen; *oil well* Ölquelle

wet [wet] 11 *the wet end of the paper machine* die Naßpartie der Papiermaschine (= *der Teil der Papiermaschine, in dem sich das Papierblatt bildet und das Wasser entzogen wird*)

wheel [wiːl] 1 Rad

wheel clamp [ˈwiːl ˈklæmp] 17 Parkkralle

whiten [ˈwaɪtn] 12 weiß machen; weißen

winch [wɪntʃ] 9 *(hier:)* Winde; *(auch:)* Kurbel

wind [waɪnd] 12 (wound [waʊnd] – have wound) wickeln; winden; aufspulen; *the dried paper is wound onto vast reels* das getrocknete Papier wird auf riesige Rollen gewickelt; *wind a hose* einen Schlauch aufwickeln

winding tracks [ˈwaɪndɪŋ] T1 gewundene (verschlungene) Wege

wire [ˈwaɪə] 3/12 Draht; *the wire of a paper machine* das Sieb einer Papiermaschine

wire gauze [ˈwaɪə ˈgɔːz] 11 Drahtgeflecht

within [wɪˈðɪn] 16 innerhalb

wonder [ˈwʌndə] 4/6 sich fragen; *I wonder if this is correct* ich frage mich, ob das richtig ist

List of common irregular verbs

arise – arose – arisen
awake – awoke/awaked – awoken/awaked

bear – bore – borne
beat – beat – beaten, beat
become – became – become
begin – began – begun
bend – bent – bent
bet – bet/betted – bet/betted
bid – bad(e)/bid – bid/bidden
bind – bound – bound
bite – bit – bitten, bit
bleed – bled – bled
blow – blew – blown
break – broke – broken
breed – bred – bred
bring – brought – brought
broadcast – broadcast – broadcast
build – built – built
burn – burnt/burned – burnt/burned
burst – burst – burst
buy – bought – bought

cast – cast – cast
catch – caught – caught
choose – chose – chosen
cling – clung – clung
come – came – come
cost – cost – cost
creep – crept – crept
cut – cut – cut

deal – dealt – dealt
deepfreeze – deepfroze – deepfrozen
dig – dug – dug
dive – dived (*US also* dove) – dived
do – did – done
draw – drew – drawn
dream – dreamt/dreamed – dreamt/dreamed
drink – drank – drunk
drive – drove – driven
dwell – dwelt/dwelled – dwelt/dwelled

eat – ate – eaten
fall – fell – fallen
feed – fed – fed
feel – felt – felt
fight – fought – fought
find – found – found
flee – fled – fled
fling – flung – flung
fly – flew – flown
forbid – forbade/forbad – forbidden
forget – forgot – forgotten, forgot
forgive – forgave – forgiven
forsake – forsook – forsaken
freeze – froze – frozen

get – got – got (*US also* gotten)
give – gave – given
go – went – gone
grind – ground – ground
grow – grew – grown
hang – hung/hanged – hung/hanged
have – had – had
hear – heard – heard
heave – heaved – heaved
hide – hid – hidden/hid
hit – hit – hit
hold – held – held
hurt – hurt – hurt
input – input/inputted – input/inputted
inset – inset – inset
keep – kept – kept
kneel – knelt (*US* kneeled) – knelt (*US* kneeled)
knit – knitted/knit – knitted/knit
know – knew – known
lay – laid – laid
lead – led – led
lean – leant/leaned – leant/leaned
leap – leapt/leaped – leapt/leaped
learn – learnt/learned – learnt/learned

leave – left – left
lend – lent – lent
let – let – let
lie – lay – lain
light – lit/lighted – lit/lighted
lose – lost – lost
make – made – made
mean – meant – meant
meet – met – met
mow – mowed – mown/mowed
output – output/outputted – output/outputted
overtake – overtook – overtaken

pay – paid – paid
put – put – put

read – read – read
rid – rid – rid
ride – rode – ridden
ring – rang – rung
rise – rose – risen
run – ran – run

saw – sawed – sawn (*US also* sawed)
say – said – said
see – saw – seen
seek – sought – sought
sell – sold – sold
send – sent – sent
set – set – set
sew – sewed – sewn/sewed
shake – shook – shaken
shave – shaved – shaved/shaven
shed – shed – shed
shine – shone – shone
shoot – shot – shot
show – showed – shown
shrink – shrank/shrunk – shrunk
shut – shut – shut
sing – sang – sung
sink – sank, sunk – sunk

sit – sat – sat
sleep – slept – slept
slide – slid – slid, slidden
sling – slung – slung

slit – slit – slit
smell – smelt/smelled – smelt/smelled

sow – sowed – sown, sowed
speak – spoke – spoken
speed – sped/speeded – sped/speeded
spell – spelt/spelled – spelt/spelled
spend – spent – spent
spill – spilt/spilled – spilt/spilled
spin – spun, span – spun
split – split – split
spoil – spoilt/spoiled – spoilt/spoiled
spread – spread – spread
spring – sprang – sprung
stand – stood – stood
steal – stole – stolen
stick – stuck – stuck
sting – stung – stung
stink – stank/stunk – stunk
strike – struck – struck
string – strung – strung
swear – swore – sworn
sweep – swept – swept
swell – swelled – swollen/swelled
swim – swam – swum
swing – swung – swung

take – took – taken
teach – taught – taught
tear – tore – torn
tell – told – told
think – thought – thought
throw – threw – thrown
thrust – thrust – thrust
tread – trod – trodden/trod

wake – woke – woken
wear – wore – worn
weave – wove – woven
weep – wept – wept
wet – wetted/wet – wetted/wet
win – won – won
wind – wound – wound
withdraw – withdrew – withdrawn
withstand – withstood – withstood
wring – wrung – wrung
write – wrote – written

Technical abbreviations

A	atomic weight; acre; ampere
AC/ac	alternating current
A.D.	(= anno domini) letters used before dates to show the number of years after the beginning of the Christian era; anno domini = in the year of our Lord)
Ah	ampere hour(s)
am	(ante meridiem) before noon
AM	amplitude modulation
amps	ampere
approx.	approximately
ASA	American Standards Association
a.s.a.p.	as soon as possible
ASCII	American Standard Code for Information Interchange (= standard code for storing and transmitting information in computer systems; also called character code)
ass	assembler (= program, usually provided by the computer manufacturer, to translate a program written in assembly language into machine code)
asst	assistant
assy	assembly
at/atm	atmosphere
AT	advanced technology
ATM	automatic teller machine
av	average
B & W	black and white
bbl	barrel (US barrel of 42 US gallons = 35 GB gallons: often used as a unit of capacity, especially in the oil industry ; 1 barrel = 159 litres)
bd	bone dry
BIOS	basic input and output system
BSI	British Standards Institution
Btu	British thermal unit
c	centi-
C	Centigrade
CAD	computer-aided design
CAE	computer-aided engineering
CAI	computer-aided instruction
cal	calorie
CAL	computer-aided learning
CAM	computer-aided manufacturing
CAN	complete area networks
cc	cubic centimetre(s)
CCTV	closed-circuit television
cd	candela

CD	compact disk
CD-ROM	compact-disk read-only memory (= a non-magnetic disk on which a certain number of megabytes of data can be permanently recorded by using a laser beam to burn microscopic pits into the surface)
CEO	chief executive officer
cf	(= confer) see
CGA	computer graphics adapter
ch	cheval vapeur (= French) PS (= metric horsepower)
chem	chemical
CIM	computer-integrated manufacturing
CNC	computer numerical control (= a control system in which numerical values corresponding to desired tool or control positions are generated by a computer)
cp	compare (with)
CPU	central processing unit
CRT	cathode ray tube
c/s	cycles per second
cu ft	cubic feet
CV	curriculum vitae
cwt	hundredweight
D	depth
d	deci-
da	deca-
db	decibel (= a unit for measuring the relative loudness of sounds, or for measuring power levels in electrical communications)
dc/DC	direct current
DDU	disk drive unit
dept/dpt	department
dia	diameter
DIY	do-it-yourself
DOS	disk operating system
doz	dozen
dpi	dots per inch
DTP	desktop publishing
dz	dozen
EAN	European article number
ECT	elemental chlorine-free (papermaking)
EDP	electronic data processing
eg	(= exempli gratia) for example, for instance
E-mail	electronic mail
emf	electromotive force
EPOS	electronic point of sale
EPROM	erasable programable read-only memory (= a read-only memory in which stored data can be erased by ultraviolet light or other means and reprogrammed bit by bit with voltage pulses)
etc	(= et cetera) and so on

Ext	extension
F	Fahrenheit
f	female
fig	figure
fl oz	fluid ounce
FM	frequency modulation
4WD	four-wheel drive
ft	foot/feet
G	giga-
g	acceleration due to gravity; gram
gal	gallon
GIGO	garbage in, garbage out (= expression meaning that the accuracy and quality of information that is output depends entirely on the quality of the input)
gms/m^2	grams per square metre
gr. wt.	gross weight
H	height
h	hecto-; hour
ha	hectare
HD	heavy duty
HDTV	high definition television (= television equivalent of high fidelity, in which the reproduced image contains such a large number of accurately reproduced elements that picture details approximate those of the original scene; in general, HDTV systems use 1,000 or more scanning lines)
hi-fi	hi-fidelity
hl	hectolitre
hp	horsepower
hr(s)	hour(s)
HSS	high-speed steel
Hz	hertz
IC	integrated circuit
i.e.	(= id est) that is
in(s)	inch(es)
ISDN	integrated services digital network (=a public digital communications network which has capabilities of signalling, switching, and transport over facilities such as wire pairs, coaxial cables, optical fibres, microwave radio, and satellites; it supports a wide range of services such as voice, data, video, facsimile, and music)
ISO	International Standardisation Organisation
j	joule
JIT	just in time
K	kelvin; kilo; thousand ("salary £25K+" = salary more than £25,000 per annum)
KB/kB	kilobyte
kg	kilogram
kHz	kilohertz
km	kilometre
kph	kilometres per hour

kW	kilowatt
L	length
l	litre
LAN	local area network (= a communications network connecting various hardware devices together within a building by means of a cable or an in-house voice-data telephone system)
laser	(light amplification by stimulated emission of radiation)
lb(s)	pound(s)
LCD	liquid crystal display (= a digital display consisting of two sheets of glass separated by a sealed-in, normally transparent, liquid crystal material; a voltage applied between front and back electrode coatings disrupts the orderly arrangement of the molecules, darkening the liquid enough to form visible characters even though no light is generated)
LED	light emitting diode (= a semiconductor diode that converts electric energy into electromagnetic radiation at visible and near-infrared wavelengths)
l/min	litre(s) per minute
LPG	liquified/liquid petroleum gas
ltr	litre
LQ	letter quality
LWC	light-weight coated (paper)
m	metre; milli; male
MAN	metropolitan area network
max	maximum
MB/Mb	megabyte
mb	millibar
mf	machine finished (papermaking)
mg	milligram
MHz	megahertz
mi	mile(s)
min	minimum
MIPS	millions of instructions per second
ml	millilitre
mm	millimetre
m/min	metres per minute
modem	modulator/demodulator (= a combination modulator and demodulator at each end of a telephone line: it converts binary digital information to audio tone signals suitable for transmission over the telephone line, and vice versa)
mol	mole
MOS	metal oxide semiconductor
MOSFET	metal oxide semiconductor field effect transistor
NA/na	not available
NASA	National Aeronautics and Space Administration
n	nano-
NCR	no carbon required
NLQ	near letter quality

No/no	number
ns	nanosecond
NC	numeric control
nt. wt.	net weight
OCR	optical character reader
OHC	overhead camshaft (= a camshaft mounted above the cylinder head)
OHV	overhead valve (= an OHV engine is a four-stroke-cycle internal combustion engine which has its valves located in the cylinder head, operated by pushrods)
oz	ounce
p	pico-
Pa	pascal
PA	personal assistant; public address system
PC	personal computer; printed circuit
pc	per cent
PCW	post consumer waste
PIN	personal identification number
pkg	package
PLC	public limited company; programmable logic controller
pm	(= post meridiem) afternoon
PO Box	post office box
POS	point of sale
pp	pages
ppm	parts per million
psi	pounds per square inch
PTO/pto	please turn over
pt	pint; point
PVC	polyvinyl chloride
qt	quart
qty	quantity
r	radius
rad	radian
R & D	research and development
RAM	random access memory (= a computer memory which can be read and changed by the programmer; it is usually made on a chip; each storage location can be identified by co-ordinates)
re	referring to
REM	roentgen equivalent man (= a unit of radiation, equal to the amount that produces the same damage to humans as 1 roentgen of high-voltage x-rays)
rev/min	revolutions per minute
RISC	reduced instruction set computer
roro	roll-on roll-off
rpm	revolutions per minute
RV	recreational vehicle (eg motorhome, caravan)
s	second
SC	supercalendered (papermaking)

sec	second
sect	section
spec(s)	specifications
st	steradian
SWG	Imperial Standard Wire Gauge
t	ton; tonne
TCF	total chlorine free (papermaking)
temp	temporary
t/h	tons per hour
UHF	ultra high frequency
UV	ultraviolet
VAT	value-added tax
VCR	video cassette recorder
VDU	visual display unit
VGA	video graphics array
VHF	very high frequency
viz	(= videlicet) namely
vol	volume
W	watt; width
WAN	wide area network (= a system of interconnected computers that generally covers a large geographic area)
whd	width, height and depth
wpm	words per minute
wt	weight
WYSIWYG	what you see is what you get (= after working on the screen of a VDU, the user can print exactly what appears on the screen)
yd(s)	yard(s)

SI – The International System of Units (1)

● **Nine basic units**

metre m LENGTH	The SI unit of area is the square metre (m^2). The SI unit of volume is the cubic metre (m^3).
kilogram kg MASS	The standard for the kilogram is a cylinder of platinum-iridium alloy kept by the International Bureau of Weights and Measures at Paris.
second s TIME	A second is defined in terms of the resonance vibration of the caesium-133 atom. Symbols: ″ = second; ′ = minute
ampere A ELECTRIC CURRENT	1 ampere hour = unit of charge, equal to 3,600 coulombs, or 1 ampere flowing for 1 hour
kelvin K TEMPERATURE	The kelvin is defined as the fraction 1/273.16 of the thermo-dynamic temperature of the triple point of water. The temperature 0 K is called "absolute zero".
mole mol AMOUNT OF SUBSTANCE	The mole ist the amount of substance of a system that contains as many elementary entities as there are atoms in 0.012 kilo gram of carbon 12.
candela cd LUMINOUS INTENSITY	The SI unit of light flux is the lumen (lm). A 100-watt light bulb emits about 1700 lumens
radian rad PLANE ANGLE	The radian is the SI unit of plane angular measure. $2\pi\ \text{rad} = 360°$ $1° = \frac{\pi}{180}\ \text{rad}$
steradian sr SOLID ANGLE	The steradian is the solid angle subtended at the centre of a sphere by an area on its surface equal to the square of the radius. ONE STERADIAN

SI – The International System of Units (2)

● **Nine units derived from basic units**

joule J WORK AND ENERGY	Joule is the work done when the point of application of 1 newton is displaced through a distance of 1 metre in the direction of the force. 1 cal (non-SI unit) = 4.18680 J
newton N FORCE	One newton is the force which, when applied to a 1 kilogram mass, will give the kilogram mass an acceleration of 1 metre per second per second. 1 N m (= newton metre) = 1 J
hertz Hz FREQUENCY	Hertz indicates the number of cycles per second; a periodic oscillation has a frequency of n hertz if in 1 second it goes through n cycles.
pascal Pa PRESSURE AND STRESS	One pascal is the pressure produced by a force of 1 newton applied over an area of 1 square metre. $1 \text{ N/m}^2 = 1$ Pa / 1 bar $= 10^5$ Pa
metre per second m/s VELOCITY	This is the time rate of change of position of a body; it is a vector quantity having direction as well as magnitude. 1 foot per second (ft/s) = 0.3048 m/s
watt W POWER	One watt is the power which gives rise to the energy of 1 joule in 1 second. 1 J = 1 N m = 1 Ws 1 Wh $= 3.6 \times 10^3$ J
bar bar PRESSURE AND STRESS	Bar is a unit of pressure or stress. 1 bar $= 10^5 \text{ N/m}^2$ or pascals = 750.07 mm of mercury at 0°C and latitude 45°. 1 millibar (mbar) $= 100 \text{ N/m}^2$
ohm Ω RESISTANCE	Ohm is the SI unit of electrical resistance: 1 ampere through it produces a potential difference across it of 1 volt. $1 \, \Omega = 1$ V/A
volt v ELECTROMOTIVE FORCE	Volt is the difference of electrical potential between two points of a conducting wire carrying a constant current of 1 ampere; the power dissipated between these points is equal to 1 watt.

British and American weights and measures

Length
inch (in) = 2.5399 centimetres
12 inches = 1 foot (ft)
3 feet (ft) = 1 yard (yd)
1,760 yards = 1 mile (mi) = 1,609.3 metres

Area
1 square inch (in^2) = 6.452 square centimetres
144 square inches = 1 square foot (ft^2)
9 square feet = 1 square yard (yd^2)
4,840 square yards = 1 acre = 0.4047 hectare
640 acres = 1 square mile (mi^2) = 259 hectares

Weight
ounce (oz) = 28.3495 grams
16 ounces = 1 pound (lb) = 453.59 grams

(GB): 112 pounds = 1 hundredweight (cwt) = 50.80 kilograms
2,240 pounds = 1 long ton = 1,016.05 kilograms

(US): 100 pounds = 1 hundredweight (cwt) = 45.36 kilograms
2,000 pounds = 1 short ton = 907.18 kilograms

Cubic measure
1 cubic inch (in^3) = 16.387 cubic centimetres
1,728 cubic inches = 1 cubic foot (ft^3)
27 cubic feet = 1 cubic yard (yd^3) = 0.7646 cubic metre

Liquid measure
(GB): 1 pint = 0.568 litre
2 pints = 1 quart
4 quarts = 1 imperial gallon = 4.546 litres

(US): 1 pint = 0.4732 litre
2 pints = 1 quart
4 quarts = 1 gallon = 3.7853 litres

Approximate conversions from metric measures

Symbol	When You Know	Multiply by	To Find	Symbol
		LENGTH		
mm	millimeters	0.04	inches	in
cm	centimeters	0.4	inches	in
m	meters	3.3	feet	ft
m	meters	1.1	yards	yd
km	kilometers	0.6	miles	mi
		AREA		
cm^2	square centimeters	0.16	square inches	in^2
m^2	square meters	1.2	square yards	yd^2
km^2	square kilometers	0.4	square miles	mi^2
ha	hectares (10,000 m^2)	2.5	acres	
		MASS (weight)		
g	grams	0.035	ounces	oz
kg	kilograms	2.2	pounds	lb
t	tonnes (1000 kg)	1.1	short tons	
		VOLUME		
ml	milliliters	0.03	fluid ounces	fl oz
l	liters	2.1	pints	pt
l	liters	1.06	quarts	qt
l	liters	0.26	gallons	gal
m^3	cubic meters	35	cubic feet	ft^3
m^3	cubic meters	1.3	cubic yards	yd^3

Approximate conversions to metric measures

Symbol	When You Know	Multiply by	To Find	Symbol
		LENGTH		
in	inches	2.54	centimeters	cm
ft	feet	30	centimeters	cm
yd	yards	0.9	meters	m
mi	miles	1.6	kilometers	km
		AREA		
in^2	square inches	6.5	square centimeters	cm^2
ft^2	square feet	0.09	square meters	m^2
yd^2	square yards	0.8	square meters	m^2
mi^2	square miles	2.6	square kilometers	km^2
	acres	0.4	hectares	ha
		MASS (weight)		
oz	ounces	28	grams	g
lb	pounds	0.45	kilograms	kg
	short tons (2000 lb)	0.9	tonnes	t
		VOLUME		
tsp	teaspoons	5	milliliters	ml
Tbsp	tablespoons	15	milliliters	ml
fl oz	fluid ounces	30	milliliters	ml
c	cups	0.24	liters	l
pt	pints	0.47	liters	l
qt	quarts	0.95	liters	l
gal	gallons	3.8	liters	l
ft^3	cubic feet	0.03	cubic meters	m^3
yd^3	cubic yards	0.76	cubic meters	m^3

Tyre pressure in English-speaking countries

USA/GB: psi = pounds per square inch (also: lbf/in^2 = pound force per square inch)

Canada: kPa = kilopascal

Australia: psi and bar

1 psi $(= lbf/in^2) = 684.76$ Pa $= 6.894\ 76$ kN/m^2 $(= kPa) = 0.068\ 947\ 6$ bar

1 bar $= 10^5$ N/m^2 $(= 100,000$ newton per square metre$) = 14.5$ psi

concrete example: 1.9 bar = 27.55 psi = 190 kPa

Temperature in Celsius and Fahrenheit

Symbol	When You Know	Multiply by	To Find	Symbol
$°F$	Fahrenheit temperature	5/9 (after subtracting 32)	Celsius temperature	$°C$
$°C$	Celsius temperature	9/5 (then add 32)	Fahrenheit temperature	$°F$

A look at the figure "0"

zero	In saying a number, *zero* is usually used in science: *The temperature often falls below zero here. It was twelve degrees below zero. This makes the function equal to zero.*
nought	In normal conversation, *nought* is often used by British speakers (not by Americans): *There are three noughts in 6,000. A million is followed by six noughts (1,000,000). Ten minus ten is nought. Eight point nought five (8.05).*
O [əu]	In telephone or hotel room numbers, for instance, people often use *O: Her telephone number is eight-O-six-O-four (80604). Their phone number is O-double six-four-double O-three (0664003). I think he's in room six-O-nine (609).*
nil **nothing** **love**	In speaking about the score in a team game, *nil* or *nothing* are used: *The final score was four nil or four nothing (4-0). England won 3-nil.*
	In tennis, *love* is used to express "no score": *The score on the Centre Court is thirty-love (30-0).*

Instead of *nought, O* and *nil/nothing,* American speakers normally use *zero*.

Guide to English pronunciation

[ə]	number ['nʌmbə]	etwa wie *e* in *bitte*
[eə]	where [weə]	*a* zu [ə] gleitend
[e]	best [best]	etwa wie *e* in *fett*
[eɪ]	space [speɪs]	von [e] zu [ɪ] gleitend
[əʊ]	low [ləʊ]	von [ə] zu [ʊ] gleitend
[ɜ:]	early ['ɜ:lɪ]	etwa wie *ö* in *Segeltörn* (aber ohne *r*!)

[ʌ]	run [rʌn]	etwa wie *a* in *Matsch*
[ɑ:]	last [lɑ:st]	etwa wie *a* in *Kahn*
[aɪ]	file [faɪl]	etwa wie *ei* in *fein*
[aʊ]	brown [braʊn]	etwa wie *au* in *Bau*
[æ]	stand [stænd]	etwa wie *ä* in *lächeln*

[ɪ]	bit [bɪt]	etwa wie *i* in *mit*
[ɪə]	near [nɪə]	etwa wie *ie* in *Bier*
[i:]	beat [bi:t]	etwa wie *ie* in *Miete*

[ɒ]	lot [lɒt]	etwa wie *o* in *Grotte*
[ɔɪ]	join [dʒɔɪn]	etwa wie *eu* in *neu*
[ɔ:]	saw [sɔ:]	etwa wie *o* in *Korn* (aber ohne *r*!)

[ʊ]	book [bʊk]	etwa wie *u* in *Futter*
[ʊə]	sure [ʃʊə]	von [ʊ] zu [ə] gleitend
[u:]	tool [tu:l]	etwa wie *u* in *Buch*

[θ]	thing [θɪŋ]	etwa wie gelispeltes *ß* (*Biß*)
[ð]	that [ðæt]	etwa wie gelispeltes *s* (*Sand*)
[ʃ]	shift [ʃɪft]	etwa wie *sch* in *fesch*
[ʒ]	measure ['meʒə]	etwa wie das zweite *g* in *Garage*
[s]	service ['sɜ:vɪs]	etwa wie *ß* in *reißen*
[z]	please [pli:z]	etwa wie *s* in *Museum*

[ŋ]	wrong [rɒŋ]	etwa wie *ng* in *bang*

[r]	repeat [rɪ'pi:t]	kein gerolltes *r*! Zunge im Gaumen leicht zurückbiegen
[v]	visit ['vɪzɪt]	etwa wie *w* in *Wein*
[w]	wheel [wi:l]	zuerst wie kurzes *u* ansetzen, dann schnell zum nachfolgenden Laut übergehen

[']	collect [kə'lekt]	(deutet die stärker betonte Silbe an)

The RP *vowels and diphthongs* are transcribed as follows:

bean	barn	born	boon	burn				
iː	ɑː	ɔː	uː	ɜː				

pit	pet	pat	putt	pot	put	another		
ɪ	e	æ	ʌ	ɒ	ʊ	ə ə		

bay	buy	boy	no	now	peer	pair	poor	(pour)
eɪ	aɪ	ɔɪ	əʊ	aʊ	ɪə	eə	ʊə	ɔə

The RP *consonants* are transcribed as follows:

pin	bin	tin	din	come	gum	chain	Jane	
p	b	t	d	k	g	tʃ	dʒ	

fine	vine	think	this	seal	zeal	sheep	measure	how
f	v	θ	ð	s	z	ʃ	ʒ	h

sum	sun	sung	light	right	wet	yet		
m	n	ŋ	l	r	w	j		

Grammar and subject index

The numbers refer to the pages in the book.

The Fun They Had – words and phrases

addition [əˈdɪʃn] Addition
adjust [əˈdʒʌst] einstellen, justieren
attic [ˈætɪk] Dachstube, Mansarde
beneath [bɪˈniːθ] unter, unterhalb
betcha [ˈbetʃə] I betcha *(US:)* und ob! aber sicher!
blank out [blæŋk] *(hier:)* ausfallen
crinkly [ˈkrɪŋklɪ] zerknittert
dials [ˈdaɪəlz] Meßgeräte
diary [ˈdaɪərɪ] Tagebuch
dispute [dɪˈspjuːt] *... to dispute that ...* das zu bestreiten
flash [flæʃ] *... flashing on the screen ...* auf dem Bildschirm aufleuchten
fraction [ˈfrækʃən] *proper fractions* echte Brüche
gear [ɡɪə] *it was geared a little too quick* es war ein wenig zu schnell eingestellt
guess [ɡes] vermuten; (er)raten *I guess* nehme ich an
lofty [ˈlɒftɪ] *he added loftily (etwa:)* fügte er mit einem hochmütigen Ausdruck hinzu
mark [mɑːk] *(hier:)* Schulnote
mind [maɪnd] *it must fit the mind of each boy* es muß auf den Verstand (Kopf) eines jeden Jungen abgestimmt sein
nonchalantly [ˈnɒnʃələntlɪ] *(etwa:)* unbekümmert, lässig
pat [pæt] *he patted her head* er tätschelte ihr den Kopf
punch code [ˈpʌntʃ ˈkəʊd] Lochstreifen-Kode
scornful [ˈskɔːnfʊl] *(etwa:)* spöttisch-verächtlich
scream [skriːm] *he screamed with laughter* er schrie vor Lachen
sigh [saɪ] Seufzer
sorrowful [ˈsɒrəʊfʊl] *she shook her head sorrowfully* sie schüttelte sorgenvoll den Kopf
superior [suːˈpɪərɪə] *with very superior eyes* mit einem sehr überlegen wirkenden Ausdruck in den Augen
suppose [səˈpəʊz] vermuten, annehmen *... they were supposed to ...* wie sie es eigentlich sollten
time [taɪm] *in no time* im Nu
tuck [tʌk] *tucked beneath his arm* unter seinen Arm geklemmt
whistle [ˈwɪsl] pfeifen

Quellenverzeichnis

Wir danken den folgenden Personen, Institutionen, Unternehmen und Verlagen für die freundliche Genehmigung von Copyright-Material, soweit sie erreicht werden konnten. Sollten Rechteinhaber hier nicht aufgeführt sein, so sind wir für entsprechende Hinweise dankbar.

Seite 7	Foto und Abbildungen: British Aerospace (Military Aircraft) Limited, Preston , England
Seite 10	Foto: Edith und Albert Schmitz
Seite 11	Cartoon reproduced from Lighter Engineering by permission of Mechanical Engineering Publications, London, England
Seite 12	Winnebago Industries, Forest City, Iowa, USA
Seite 13	Abbildung und Text: Winnebago Industries, Forest City, Iowa, USA
Seite 14	Foto: Edith und Albert Schmitz
Seite 15	English Tourist Board, London, England
Seite 16	Autohomes (UK) Limited, Poole, Dorset, England
Seite 18–20	Stewart Dunn: CRAFT, DESIGN AND TECHNOLOGY, pp 40,41,47, Unwin Hyman, part of HarperCollins Publishers
Seite 20	Abbildung unten: Design (Magazine), London, England
Seite 25	Punch/Werner Lüning, Lübeck
Seite 27	Foto unten: Edith und Albert Schmitz
Seite 29	Punch/Werner Lüning, Lübeck
Seite 31	Foto: Edith und Albert Schmitz
Seite 32	Foto: Edith und Albert Schmitz
Seite 33	Kardorama Ltd., Potter's Bar, England
Seite 36	Foto: Edith und Albert Schmitz
Seite 37	Fotos: Canada Reports (Magazine), Ottawa, Canada
Seite 42/43	Fotos und Abbildung: Construction Marketing - Bethlehem Steel, Bethlehem, PA, USA
Seite 44	Fotos: Edith und Albert Schmitz
Seite 47	Babcock Contractors Limited, Crawley, England
Seite 48/49	Babcock Contractors Limited, Crawley, England
Seite 54/55	Department of Mines and Energy, South Australia, Eastwood, South Australia
Seite 56/57	The Wiggins Teape Group Limited, Basingstoke, England
Seite 60	Abbildungen nach: British Paper & Board, Swindon, England
Seite 62/63	The Wiggins Teape Group Limited, Basingstoke, England
Seite 69	Fotos: Edith und Albert Schmitz
Seite 72–77	from: "Exploring Canada" by Vivian Bowers, Nelson Canada, A Division of Thomson Canada Limited, Scarborough, Ontario, Canada
Seite 78/79	Construction Marketing - Bethlehem Steel, Bethlehem, PA, USA
Seite 84	Abbildungen: Degussa AG, Frankfurt am Main, Deutschland
Seite 85	Cartoon reproduced from Lighter Engineering by permission of Mechanical Engineering Publications, London, England
Seite 87	Fotos und Text: Degussa AG, Frankfurt am Main, Deutschland
Seite 89	Fotos: Edith und Albert Schmitz
Seite 92	Foto und Abbildung: John Deere, Mannheim, Deutschland
Seite 93	Foto: Edith und Albert Schmitz
Seite 95	John Deere, Mannheim, Deutschland
Seite 96	Abbildungen: Mannesmann Tally GmbH, Ulm, Deutschland
Seite 97	Foto und Text: Mannesmann Tally GmbH, Ulm, Deutschland
Seite 103	Foto: Kearney & Trecker GmbH, Stuttgart, Deutschland
Seite 104	Abbildung: Kearney & Trecker GmbH, Stuttgart, Deutschland
Seite 108/109	"The Fun They Had", from EARTH IS ROOM ENOUGH by Isaac Asimov. Copyright © 1957 by Isaac Asimov. Used by permission of Doubleday, a division of Bantam Doubleday Dell Publishing Group, Inc.